Harry Hakes

The Discovery of America by Christopher Columbus

Harry Hakes

The Discovery of America by Christopher Columbus

ISBN/EAN: 9783337022969

Printed in Europe, USA, Canada, Australia, Japan

Cover: Foto ©ninafisch / pixelio.de

More available books at **www.hansebooks.com**

Columbian Fair Edition.

THE
Discovery of America

BY
CHRISTOPHER COLUMBUS.

By HARRY HAKES, M. D.

God who regards time not by years, but by eternities, reserves to His own time and for His omnipotent pleasure, His chosen instruments, to discover and publish His revelations

WILKES-BARRE, PA.:
ROBERT BAUR & SON, PRINTERS.
1892.

Preface.

If the Author may be permitted to premise, that the mass of mankind in this hurrying age, will neither purchase, peruse or possess the extensive literature pertaining to the "Discovery of America;" then, he hopes the following pages may be found to contain a sufficiently full historical statement, to elucidate the great event the world is preparing to commemorate.

HARRY HAKES.

Wilkes-Barre, Pa., May 25th, 1892.

DISCOVERY OF AMERICA
BY
CHRISTOPHER COLUMBUS.

CHAPTER I.

THE general verdict of mankind, founded upon the evidences which are preserved to us, is expressed in the single uncompromising sentence: "Christopher Columbus discovered America in the year A. D. 1492." Notwithstanding such a statement of the case is not technically in accordance with the facts as they are recorded, yet it is quite certain that such an opinion has been deliberately founded, and will remain unquestioned history throughout the coming ages.

The discovery of more than one-half of the surface of our planet, with its lands and waters hitherto unknown and quite unsuspected, was, in and of itself, the greatest achievement and the grandest event in recorded history. Such discoveries must of necessity be rare, for never again, by any foreseen possibility, can so distinguished an honor fall to the happy lot of any man as we cheerfully accord to the immortal Genoese navigator.

However, in so far as Columbus was connected with the discovery of America, it was simply a princely accident—a mere incident in his unsuccessful attempt to navigate westwardly from Europe to Asia. The discovery of an intervening continent was not anticipated nor recognized when discovered. The true character of the discovery can best be understood by keeping constantly in mind the object and purpose of Columbus in his voyages to the west. The bold navigator had determined to sail across the Atlantic Ocean to the opposite shore, where, by the general opinion, the eastern coast of Asia would be found. Columbus embraced this opinion to its fullest extent. Not only did he expect to sail to Asia, but he had become convinced that the distance was only three or four thousand miles. Upon what he based such a calculation it is difficult to conceive, nor did those who so strenuously opposed his undertaking appear to have seriously challenged his computed distance. That Columbus monstrously underestimated the true circumference of the earth is abundantly evident; but upon what data or facts, or even of theory, he was led to the belief that Europe and Asia were only separated by the west, three or four thousand miles, is likely to remain unknown. The enormous error as to the circumference of the earth which he embraced, and to which he adhered to his death, led him to the discovery of a continent, which barred his voyage to Asia almost at the threshold of his journey.

Columbus did not live to learn that he had discovered a continent, or that the broad Pacific Ocean separated the land he discovered from the golden riches and splendors of the Asia he was seeking, but destined never to behold.

On the morning of the 12th of October, 1492, Columbus landed and took possession of an island to the northeast of Cuba, called by the natives Guanahani. This was the first land sighted on his first voyage. It is to this date and to this particular event that the world has rather awkwardly assigned to

Columbus the high honors of the discovery of America. Columbus, however, on his first voyage of exploration discovered several islands, among them Cuba and San Domingo. His second voyage was limited mainly to explorations of Cuba and San Domingo. On his third voyage, on the last day of July or first day of August, 1498, he discovered the main land of South America, at the mouth of the river Orinoco. This was, in fact, his first discovery of the American continent. On his fourth and last voyage he landed upon the coast of Honduras, and followed the coast to the isthmus of Darien, and returned to Spain on the 7th day of November, 1504. This, in brief, is a statement of the total personal knowledge that Columbus ever had of the American continent. He died in 1506, and years before any one distinctly knew or recognized the exact nature of his discoveries. He died honestly persisting that he had reached Asia, or, as he seems invariably to have called the whole of Asia, "The Indies."

No one then even pretended to deny him the honor. In fact, no one could. All thought upon the subject centered in the supposition that the lands discovered were the eastern extensions of Asia.

The circumference of the earth, as determined by Eratosthenes, 200 years B. C., seems to have been forgotten, or entirely overlooked, or, still more probably, was never known by Columbus and his contemporaries.

The circumference of the earth, as understood by Columbus, made no allowance for the breadth of the American continent and the Pacific Ocean. It is evident that at that time, the general understanding and belief was that the Atlantic Ocean connected or separated western Europe from eastern Asia.

So certain was Columbus that he had reached Asia, that on his second voyage, while exploring the southern coast of Cuba, on the 12th of June, 1494, he ordered Perez de Luna, the notary of his expedition, to draw up a document attesting his discovery of the main land of Asia, which was signed by all the masters, mariners and seamen of his three vessels, and sworn to in the presence of four attesting witnesses, embodying the penalty of having their tongues cut out in case they ever should say otherwise.

CHAPTER II.

BEFORE proceeding to a relation of the facts connecting the name of Columbus with the discovery of America, it seems in best order: first, to put some limit to the significance, "Discovery of America by Columbus," or to state precisely the historical boundaries of such an assertion; secondly, to state the claims of those whose partisans allege were pre-Columbian discoverers of America; and, thirdly, a chronological and historical exposition of the various theories and philosophical speculations which constituted the ground-work, and upon which the grand experiment of Columbus was based.

By adopting this method or order the true merit of Columbus becomes clearly and intelligently palpable, and his proper place in history better recognized. It will also show with greater vividness and unmistakable precision that the errors, great and small, which he embraced, the arguments he only half appreciated, the mistakes he unwittingly made, rather than scientific learning and abundant knowledge, made him but a flexible and uncertain instrument in the unconscious embrace of blind fate, good fortune, or a bountiful Providence, blindly led to the grandest geographical discovery which has ever blessed mankind.

The wording of the title-page hereof was duly considered and adopted upon careful deliberation. To assert that Columbus was the first discoverer of America would be the sum total of folly, in face of the fact that this continent had been inhabited for unknown ages. The substance of the claim indicated by the title-page is, that it is to Columbus, through whose strong faith, indomitable courage, persistent effort, and successful navigation, that Europe and the rest of the world is indebted for their first knowledge of the existence of the American continent. The grand problem or puzzle of the past ages had been as to the possibility of crossing the Atlantic. The first voyage of discovery by Columbus settled that important question for all time. From thence there was no novelty or particular merit in a trans-Atlantic voyage.

The history of the origin or primary appearance of human beings on this continent is a sealed volume, which will never be opened by the resources of human wit or wisdom. To one of two possible sources their existence in America must be ascribed: they originated or were created here, or else they were deported from some other land.

In a remote and unrecorded history of the earth it is possible that there may have existed a land connection joining the two hemispheres of our globe by either the east or west. Again, it has been thought probable that primitive navigators may have been unwillingly carried across either the Atlantic or Pacific Ocean by adverse winds, or by favoring currents, and thus this land first became peopled.

The architecture of ancient Mexico and Peru, so markedly suggestive of Egyptian origin, has suggested an ancient communion or commercial intercourse between the peoples of the eastern and western continents, the history or knowledge of which has been buried in the oblivion of ages. Even speculation upon that problem is now useless.

The old legends or stories of possible interknowledge between the continents previous to our era, or down nearly to the age of Columbus, are of no historic value, nor are they worth repeating.

CHAPTER III.

THE alleged pre-Columbian discoveries to which reference has already been made, and to which reference is now made, are, first, to a claim of comparatively recent origin: "that the Northmen discovered some portions of the northeastern coasts of America about the year A. D. 1000."

Giving the fullest credit and effect to the evidence furnished in support of such a claim that a just and fair criticism can tolerate, it may be said that it is possible that some parts of the northeasterly shores of North America were discovered by the Northmen.

It is, however, alleged that they kept up a more or less constant intercourse with the American coast for about three hundred and fifty years, during which time attempts at colonization were made, all of which resulted in complete failure and in final abandonment.

The disputable question is not as to the possibility of the Northmen having discovered the American coast. The possibility is already conceded. In fact, such a thing ought not to be considered very improbable. The real point is: " Were they on the American coast? And can the fact be established by such evidence as the nature of the case demands?" It is asserted that their claim can be established by their records. The records or writings here alluded to are called " Sagas," and consist in part of old traditions of voyages to places or regions by them designated Helluland, Markland, Vinland, etc. Islands are also mentioned, so too are mountains and rivers; but to them no names are given. The manuscripts were made from one hundred and fifty to two hundred years after the events described transpired. As the Northmen sailed without log or compass, it is found quite impossible to determine the objective points of their voyages from the descriptions given in the Sagas. It is assumed by some that their Vinland must have been in Massachusetts or Rhode Island, and that the islands were Disco, Bear Island, Newfoundland, Nantucket, etc. The main land regions have been assumed to be anywhere from Labrador to Florida. Where, then, was their Vinland? In the first place, we have simply the names of places given. Names alone are not descriptive, valueless, and without significance.

One of our latest writers says: "The point is this: Do the manuscripts which describe their voyages belong to the pre-Columbian age? If so, then the Northmen are entitled to the credit of the prior discovery of America." This seems to be a rash, an unwarranted, conclusion. The truth of the Sagas, or that they are pre-Columbian, is not in question. Precisely what is required is, to locate geographically the names of the places mentioned in the Sagas. We have better methods of determining the location of a place than by simply a name. The best evidence is required to identify places, and such as the experience of ages has determined to be requisite.

A deed of land without boundaries, and not identified by any marks or monuments, would be quite valueless.

The partisans of the Northmen have never been able to agree, from a study of the Sagas, where to locate Vinland. It has been searched for on many latitudes and various longitudes. The attempt is to find a locality to correspond with such statements as are found in the Sagas.

A coast line can be found on almost any shore to answer to, or correspond with, the vague and uncertain indications contained in the Sagas. This, in part, causes the disagreements among the students of the records. Experience has taught us that men who build with stone, and use metals for implements and weapons, are very certain to leave evidences that are quite enduring upon the ground they have occupied. If then there was any such occupation of this continent, and particularly of the Atlantic coast, as it is claimed the Sagas relate, we ought to find some trace of it upon the ground. It is much less than three hundred years since the Pilgrims first landed on the coast of Massachusetts. Since then it is very certain the face of the country has been so marked that neither the ravages of a hundred or ten thousand years can efface the same. A party of hunters or fishermen, camped in some forest or on some stream for the space of two weeks, would be quite certain to leave some tangible and long-enduring evidence of their camping. A pipe, a broken goblet, or piece of earthenware, an empty and long-suffering beer bottle, a boot heel, buckle or button, a few stones placed for a seat or around a spring, a fireplace of stone showing the marks of fire, an old knife or spoon, or some such relic, would constitute a tell-tale long enduring and unmistakable. Some such evidence would be much more satisfactory and convincing than their exaggerated narratives and stories, with the added embellishments of twenty generations, concerning the dimensions and ferocity of a huge bear alleged to have been killed after a fierce and sanguinary struggle, or the size of a monstrous trout that was hooked, but not quite landed.

From the remotest period of history a claim of discovery or proprietorship of lands must be manifested by monuments and marks upon the lands claimed. A stake driven in the ground, a heaping up of stones, the blazing of a tree, the erection of a building, the raising of a flag, or some similar manifestation, is required to give public notice of the claim made.

But the Northmen left neither chart, mark nor monument to proclaim discovery, possession, conquest or occupation of any part of America. They were familiar with the use and manufacture of metals, had metal implements and weapons; but upon American soil no tangible evidences have been found to fortify a belief that they ever landed upon the American coasts.

In whatever other region they ever set their feet they have left enduring and unmistakable evidences of their occupation.

It would seem to have been the proper time to publicly assert their American claim at the time of discovery, or at least on the return of the Cabots and Columbus from their American voyages. Most certainly Europe never heard of such a claim until two centuries had elapsed from the American voyages of Columbus, nor until the Cabots, Corterial, Verrazzano and a host of navigators had voyaged the whole northeastern regions of America over and over again, and made charts of the coast. Conceding then the possibility of the Northmen's discovery, we must nevertheless say it profited neither themselves nor any one else anything, nor were they—Europe or the world—the better or wiser therefor.

Several recent publications upon the subject are emphasized by a decided hostility to Columbus.

The righteous and impartial judgment of mankind upon the various and conflicting claims made has long since been pronounced, while the spontaneous and world-wide efforts now being put forth for an international commemoration in honor of Columbus, as the discoverer of America, may possibly have a tendency to convince the over-zealous partisans of other claimants that the world is little inclined to reverse an opinion so long and so universally entertained upon the subject.

CHAPTER IV.

IN this connection a reference to a claim of pre-Columbian discovery of America by the partisans of Americus Vespucius cannot be overlooked. This claim is supposed to be somewhat enhanced or fortified by the circumstance that his name became attached to the newly-discovered continent. Vespucius himself never made a definite or distinct claim as a pre-Columbian discoverer of America. Nevertheless, the origin of such a claim, whether wittingly or otherwise made, is, however, apparently traced to Vespucius himself.

To understand the pertinence of the facts involved in this claim it is necessary to bear in mind that Columbus discovered the West India Islands in October, 1492, but that he did not discover the main land of the continent until July 31st, 1498, while performing his third voyage of discovery. The only evidence which has ever been adduced to prove that Vespucius discovered the continent of America before Columbus is an alleged letter claimed to have been written by him in 1504 to Piero Soderini, an old friend and schoolmate, living in Italy. His claim, therefore, rests solely upon his own alleged letter, unsupported and uncorroborated in any and every particular. The claim, said to have been set forth in the alleged letter, is: "That he sailed with a fleet of four vessels from Spain, May 10th, 1497, under the commission of King Ferdinand, and that he discovered the South American coast, at Parias, on or about the 20th of June following." It is said that in the letter he claimed to have made four voyages to the new lands, and to have given an account of his four voyages in like manner to his old friend.

He certainly did make an American voyage in 1499 to the South American coast, concerning which there is abundant corroborative proofs and no dispute, although he was not the commander of the expedition, having sailed in a subordinate capacity. The only alleged voyage pertinent to our present purpose, and which is and has been the subject of vehement dispute, is the asserted voyage of 1497, otherwise called his first voyage. The evidence of such a voyage is unsatisfactory, unconvincing, and is not conceded by the best authorities. Extensive and abundant search has been made for the original letter, and for the alleged commission for the said voyage, among the records and archives of the Government; but neither the letter nor the commission, nor any allusion to any such document, nor any mention nor any reference to any such voyage, has ever been found. No report of any such voyage has ever been found or alluded to in any private letters, papers or public documents. In the entire absence of any real, possible, or probable corroborative evidence of what must have been an open, public, notorious voyage or transaction, it has seemed quite too absurd a proposition to be generally credited. The negative evidence is so overwhelming that the better opinion seeks rather for some error or mistake than in forgery or fraud to account for such a claim. Perhaps the best solution of the matter which can be suggested is: that the claim was an after-thought of some one (possibly innocently enough) to sustain by implication an argument that Vespucius was the first discoverer of the main land, because his name had been first suggested for the new lands in 1507, by a little anonymous geographical publication emanating from the College of St. Die in the Vosges Mountains. The question in dispute will probably never be settled to the entire satisfaction of everybody. In any event, the claims for Vespucius and for the Cabots (presently to be mentioned) rest upon substantially the same foundation. We ought not to feel very sure that our opinions upon the merits of the case are of more value than the opinions of the men who lived at the time, and were actors and participants in the transactions. After the death of his father, and of Vespucius also, Diego Columbus, in 1512, brought an action against the Spanish Crown, as heir of his father, to be put in possession of the dignities, prerogatives, titles and revenues granted by the sovereigns to his father and his heirs, and also to the government of certain provinces on the Pearl coast of the continent of South America. The Government put in the plea for a defence "that those countries were not first discovered by Columbus, and that, therefore, the claim of Diego was not valid." More than one hundred witnesses were examined, but the name of Vespucius was not even mentioned. If Vespucius made the alleged discovery in 1497, it would have constituted a perfect defence to the action of Diego against the Crown, and it is more than suggestive that the King availed himself of no such defence. Diego Columbus won his case against the Crown, and thus proved his father to have been the first discoverer of South America. Many of the witnesses, as well as the King himself, had enjoyed every opportunity of knowing all the facts of the case, and it seems rashly imprudent now to ignore the judgment then solemnly rendered. The exact question in issue was as to the first discovery of Paria, or the Pearl coast, which involved all there is in the claim of Vespucius as a pre-Columbian discoverer. The question was determined by a competent court of public justice, and by its judgment we ought to abide.

It was not until 1514 to 1517 that the name America first appeared upon the charts of the newly-discovered land. At that time both Columbus and Vespucius were dead.

Las Cassas, who was acquainted with both Columbus and Vespucius, seems to have thought that the naming of the new land was an intentional fraud upon Columbus by Vespucius. He was certainly laboring under an erroneous impression, for Vespucius never made any suggestion as to the naming, and had been dead some two to five years before his name was first given to the land. At first the name was applied only to a portion of South America, which had been explored by Vespucius in 1499. Later, when North America had become more explored, the name appeared upon Mercator's map (1541) as "Ame" upon North America, and "Rica" upon South America. Finally, the name "America" was extended to cover and embrace the whole American continent, north and south.

Columbus and his partisans were barred from suggesting a name, for the reason that he insisted that the lands were the Indies. During his lifetime, and for many subsequent years, the "Indies" was the name universally applied in referring to the new discovery. There first appeared some propriety in giving the newly-discovered land a new or distinct name, in the latter part of the year 1513, after Balboa had from the Peak of Darien discovered the great waters of the Pacific Ocean, which settled the question at once that the land was no part of Asia or India. Humboldt was therefore right in concluding that it was accident and not fraud that attached the name of "America."

Since these pages were written there has been published an excellent work, "The Discovery of America," by John Fiske, in which he contends that in the original letter of Vespucius to Soderini, concerning his first voyage (1497), he speaks of a locality he visited to the west of Yucatan, called by the natives "Lariab," which by an abominable error or mistake in translation, proof-reading, or printing, in the book published at St. Die, the word "Parias" appears instead of "Lariab." Paria, or Parias, designated the Pearl coast of South America, in the region of the mouth of the river Orinoco. It was the exact question in issue as to the first discovery of "Paria," and not any other locality, that was to be decided in the lawsuit between Diego Columbus and the Crown. Paria and Lariab are localities separated by 2400 miles.

If this explanation is correct, it abundantly shows why the alleged discovery of Paria by Vespucius, in 1497, was not set up by King Ferdinand to defeat the claim of Diego Columbus. Thus Vespucius, in fact, made no claim to having discovered Paria in his letter to Soderini, for he used the word "Lariab," and not "Paria." This explanation of Mr. Fiske, however, decides nothing as to the first discovery of the main land, unless it is that the expedition on which Vespucius sailed did discover main land in 1497 at Honduras and Yucatan a year before Columbus discovered Paria and the Pearl coast. It can, however, only be a poorly concealed hostility to Columbus that furnishes the ponderous cheek to thrust upon either Vespucius or the Cabots the distinguished honor of first discoverers of America, a distinction they were too honest and too honorable to claim or assert.

CHAPTER V.

THE next and last claim put forth which it seems necessary to notice is: "That John and Sebastian Cabot were pre-Columbian discoverers of America." It is somewhat remarkable that at this late day such a claim is put forth in face of the fact that the Cabots themselves never claimed any such distinction.

The venom which pursues the fame of Columbus will not rest or be satisfied until a pre-Columbian discoverer is somewhere found. First, the claim is made in the most positive terms for the Northmen, then for Vespucius, and finally the Cabots are summoned to the assault. In the second edition of B. F. DeCosta's publication, 1890, entitled "The pre-Columbian Discovery of America, by the Northmen," not quite satisfied to risk their claims upon the evidences furnished, we read on page six of Preface: "This work is not issued with any intention of seeking to detract from the glory of the achievements of Columbus, though we should remember that the time is rapidly approaching when history will summon us to honor the Cabots, the great fellow-countrymen of the Genoese, who saw the continent of America before Columbus himself viewed it." The latter part of this sentence is decidedly stale news. During the last 390 years no one has ever disputed the fact. That the Cabots, under commission of King Henry VII, of England, sailed from Bristol, England, in the good ship Matthew, and discovered the northeastern coasts of America, in the region of Newfoundland, a little more than a year before Columbus saw the main land of South America, is true; but before crediting them "pre-Columbian discoverers of America," let them speak for themselves. It is manifest that they were highly honorable men, and modest in speaking of their navigations. In a conversation with the Pope's envoy, in Spain, Sebastian Cabot says: "When news were brought that Don Christopher Colonus (Genoese) had discovered the coasts of India, whereof was great talk in all the Court of King Henry VII, who then reigned, insomuch that all men with great admiration affirmed it to be a thing more divine than human to sail by the west into the east, where spices grow, by a map that was never known before—by this fame and report there increased in my heart a great flame of desire to attempt some notable thing." Thus we see the notable thing or voyage he contemplated and performed was entirely secondary to the great first voyage of Columbus, which all men (himself included) thought rather a divine than human exploit in navigation. If the discovery of the main land by Vespucius, in 1497, is conceded, no more merit could attach to it than to the discovery by the Cabots. Cabot, like a generous, honorable man, gives the reason and the prompting for his voyage. Certainly, Vespucius could give no better reason, had he felt so disposed to do. There seems, therefore, no urgent necessity, at this particular period, for Mr. DeCosta to notify us that "history will soon summon us to honor the Cabots," etc. However, it is presumed the world will be in readiness to honor the Cabots whenever the summons is served. The Cabots were not only honorable, but brave men, and never, so far as is known, begged of Columbus a share in the honors pertaining to the discovery of the new world.

That it was the first daring voyage of Columbus, and his discovery of land in the depths of the Atlantic, which led to the discovery of our continent soon afterward, upon which is based "The Discovery of America by Columbus," is quite apparent, rather than the actual continental discovery, whether by Vespucius or the Cabots, in 1497, or of Columbus, in 1498. Had the real character, magnitude and significance of the first discoveries been at the time known or understood, there cannot be a doubt that the whole continent and islands would have been rightly and promptly christened Columbia.

Therefore the general judgment of the civilized world, upon a candid consideration of all of the facts of the case, is generous, righteous and just.

CHAPTER VI.

IMBUED with a proper admiration, and possibly a rather fervent enthusiasm for the great Genoese navigator, there are potent reasons at this time why we should recall the history of the discovery of our continent from the depths of time, and refresh our memory with the labors and contributions of the ancient world, in studying the problems that made the voyages of Columbus apparently feasible and possible. We cannot conceive that thinking men could be forever content to dwell on this earth without first or last experiencing a curiosity or desire to ascertain its extent and form. At what early age such a desire was first manifested history fails to inform us.

It was the proper business of the people inhabiting this earth to ascertain its dimensions and form—to search out and utilize the lands and waters upon its surface. This was not the work of a day, year, or of a thousand years, as we well know. Nor yet was it to be the result of the labors of one man or of one nation or age.

To correctly estimate or appreciate the noble and heroic part performed to this desirable end and intent by the subject of this dissertation, let us bring before our minds in brief review the various steps or processes of speculation, theories, reasonings and demonstrations which paved the way for one who possessed the faith and courage to attempt the demonstration of a problem that to his day rested only upon deductions from theory or the speculations of the philosopher. If the earth were really round, the proposition of Columbus to sail west to Asia was feasible. The question thus hinged upon the sphericity of the earth. The sphericity of the earth was not apparent to the common sense of the ancient world. It certainly was no popular theory in the age of Columbus, nor would it be now except for the actual demonstration made since 1519.

Even the voyages and discoveries made by Columbus, did not demonstrate the possibility of circumnavigating the earth, or of themselves sufficiently demonstrate the earth to be a sphere. That great event awaited a Magellan, not many years later.

Astronomers had become satisfied of the sphericity of the earth long before attempts were made to estimate its size. The Egyptians and Chinese were pioneers in astronomical observations, but their records give no intimation of even a suspicion that the figure of the earth is spherical. We call to mind no passage in the Old Testament, or in the later sacred writings, indicative of the spherical form of the earth. In fact, the phrases, "face of the earth," and "ends of the earth," indicate simply the early Greek idea of the earth, to wit: a disc, the popular idea and representation, as late and later than the era of Columbus.

In brief chronological order let us enumerate some of the leading theories and proofs which Columbus found at hand to fortify him in his belief that he could navigate to China by a voyage westward from Europe. Not that we can assert that Columbus was aware of all that was or had been known, or that he entirely appreciated all the ancient arguments and theories. Very certain he did not.

About 1000 years B. C., Homer speaks of the earth with its circumfluent ocean. This is not a very definite geodetic representation, but embodied the original Greek disc-earth, a plane, and surrounded by an ocean. About 600 years B. C., Thales, of Miletus, recognized as a very wise man, and founder of the Ionian School of Philosophy, is said to have believed the earth to be globular or spherical in form. This is the earliest intimation we have been able to find pertaining to the matter; and if he was in fact the first man to possess such an idea, we may agree with his countrymen that he was a very wise man.

Some 530 years B. C., Pythagoras, of the Ionian School of Philosophy, in Italy, taught publicly that the earth was in form spherical, and was the center of the solar system; but to a select coterie of his disciples he taught, privately, that the sun was the center of the solar system, and that the earth moved around the sun. Most certainly he must have had the best idea of all the ancient philosophers regarding the bodies and movements of the solar system. More than 2000 years later, Copernicus, with greater opportunities and additional evidences, perfected the Pythagorean theory of the relative positions and movements of the bodies of the solar system.

About 520 years B. C., Anaximander, a successor of Thales at the school at Miletus, is said to have thought the earth cylindrical in form. It seems reasonable to doubt, if this translation gives us the real idea of that distinguished philosopher. Philolaus, of Crotona, a disciple of Pythagoras, believed, like his master, that the earth was a sphere. Nicetas seems to have been one of the first philosophers who dared to publicly teach the theory of Pythagoras. Heraclides, of Pontus, and Ecphantus, disciples of Pythagoras, were the first to teach the revolution of the earth upon its axis, causing the apparent motion of the stars. About the same time, Eudoxus, of Cnidus, is said to have held the earth to be a sphere, from observing the differing altitudes of the stars from different points on the earth's surface.

Three hundred and fifty years B. C., Aristotle, a distinguished philosopher and the father of the modern methods of demonstrations in the exact sciences, an astronomer, geographer and cosmographer, of great authority in his age, speaks of the sphericity of the earth as a matter generally agreed upon by the learned astronomers of his day. About 326 years B. C., Pythias, of Marseilles, made the first attempts to utilize the resources of astronomy in aid of geographic representation. He was a distinguished navigator, and voyaged as far north as Iceland, then known as "Thule," or "Ultima Thule."

Dicærchus, a pupil of Aristotle, about 310 years B. C., made the first approach to a modern projection of the earth—a first attempt toward the construction of maps and charts, representing the surface of the earth.

Two hundred years before our era, Ptolemy Euergetus, called Eratosthenes to the care and superintendence of the renowned Alexandrian library. As Thales appears to deserve the high honor of first announcing the sphericity of the earth, so likewise Eratosthenes appears a pioneer to demonstrate, upon correct principles, the magnitude and circumference of the earth. He was discreet enough to adopt the method which modern science has fully approved. He appears to have assumed that Syene, one of the most southern cities of ancient Egypt, was situated upon the same meridian as Alexandria. He therefore conceived the idea of determining the amplitude of the celestial arc, intercepted between the zeniths of the two places, and of measuring at the same time their distances apart on the ground—operations which would furnish the data for the determination of the entire length of the terrestrial meridian or total circumference of the earth. Syene was known to be situated exactly under the Tropic of Cancer, for on the day of the summer solstice the sun cast his rays to the bottom of a deep well in that city. Eratosthenes also had observed that on the day of the solstice the meridional distance of the sun from the zenith of Alexandria to be seven degrees and twelve minutes—the fiftieth part of 360 degrees, and the fiftieth part of the circumference of the earth. The surveyors of Alexander and the Ptolemys had determined that the itinerary distance between Syene and Alexandria was 5000 stadia; therefore the distance,

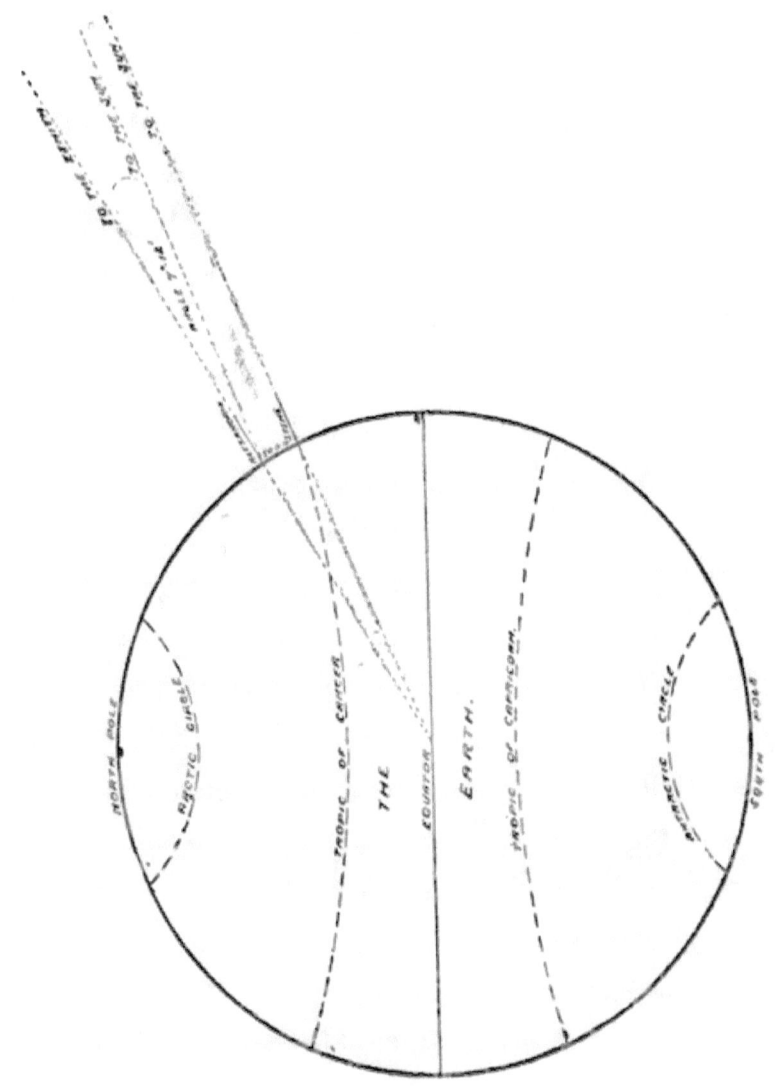

multiplied by fifty, gave 250,000 stadia for the circumference of the earth. It has been objected that we cannot know with much precision what the distance or circumference was determined to be, as we are not certain as to the length of the standard or stade he used. To some extent this is so. But the distance between Syene and Alexandria is and was substantially 500 miles; therefore, by dividing his numbers by ten, gives us 500 miles, and 25,000 miles. This makes the circumference 160 miles too much, and yet the error, for the purposes of circumnavigating the earth, would be of but little moment. It may, for our purposes herein, be assumed that ten stadia represented one English mile. While we may not know the exact length of the stadia used, we may, nevertheless, feel certain that the distance between Alexandria and Syene is the same that it was 2000 years ago. In fact, Syene passed the meridian about ten minutes ahead of Alexandria; but even that error would change the result but a mere fraction.

A century and a half B. C., Hipparchus, a learned astronomer and skilled mathematician, laid down the true rule and guide for correct geographic representation, to wit: by a determination of the latitude and longitude of places. He discarded entirely the estimated distances of travelers.

Near this period, Crates, of Mallus, made (so far as we can ascertain) the first artificial globe. On this he delineated the surface of the earth as he guessed it to be.

CHAPTER VII.

ABOUT the year 75 A. D., Marinus, of Tyre, made an attempt to construct a map of such portions of the earth's surface as he had some knowledge about upon the plan suggested by Hipparchus, and added such portions as he had heard about from travelers. His map was known by Columbus through Ptolemy. The monstrous error it contained in making the distance east from the Canary Islands to the east coast of China 225 degrees of longitude, as well as a smaller error on the map of Ptolemy, next to be mentioned, led Columbus into the enormous error of supposing he could come to the eastern Asiatic coast by a voyage to the west of three thousand to four thousand miles. It is not unsupposable that a daring and courageous navigator might undertake a voyage of three or four thousand miles, over an unknown and dreaded sea, who would hesitate at a voyage of 14,490 miles.

Claudius Ptolemy, the greatest geographer of his

time, made his observations at Alexandria, and between the years 127 to 150 of our era put forth his geographical conclusions upon a map which, until the time of Columbus, remained an authority among the learned. In him were combined the elements of learning absolutely essential for a geographer, to wit: a knowledge of astronomy and mathematics. As his almagest continued an authority among the learned for many centuries, so likewise his geography continued the best exposition upon that subject, until it was displaced and superceded by the progress of maritime discovery in the fifteenth and sixteenth centuries. Like his predecessor, Marinus, he attempted to construct his map upon the plan suggested by Hipparchus, to wit: by determination of the latitude and longitude of places, so as to exhibit their relative positions and distances and directions one from the other. Ptolemy was so well pleased with the work of Marinus that he used it as a basis for his own in many respects, particularly (as he says) for those regions bordering upon the Mediterranean Sea.

Both Marinus and Ptolemy failed to appreciate or

concede the computations of Eratosthenes and Strabo as to the magnitude or circumference of the earth, to wit: about 25,000 miles. As a result it distorted all the relative positions and distances of places. Of course, they, as well as Eratosthenes and Strabo, computed the circumference of the earth by the Babylonian sexagesimal system of 360 degrees to complete the great circle. But they assumed that the known world from the Canary Islands (their prime meridian) by the east to Quinsay, the eastern coast of China, covered or embraced, according to Ptolemy, 180 degrees, and, according to Marinus, 225 degrees, while the real distance is but 130 degrees (8190 miles). This was favorable to the project of Columbus, for the greater the known distance the shorter would be the unknown distance. Their great error is palpable upon inspection of the map of Ptolemy, by his endeavor to extend the European and Asiatic longitudes east to 180 degrees, when they are embraced within 130 degrees. Thus the Mediterranean Sea appeared 600 miles longer than it is. Of course this fundamental error extended to his whole delineation. A large portion of his map was pure conjecture. It had been a fixed belief of all the Greek geographers that the earth was about twice as broad from east to west as from north to south. Though it was a pure assumption, it took so firm a hold upon the minds of men that even Marinus and Ptolemy show us by their maps that they were imbued with the common error.

There can be no doubt that the undue extension of Asia to the east, so as to diminish by about seventy-five to ninety degrees of longitude the interval between that continent and the western coasts of Europe, had a material or possibly a controlling influence in fostering the belief of Toscanelli, Columbus, and others, that it was possible to reach the land of spices by a short voyage to the west.

To sum up the value of the real knowledge of this prince of geographers, and the value of his map to Columbus, we must bear in mind that Iceland was his northerly limit for Europe; that the Atlantic shores limited him as to the west; that the western coast of Africa, from Cape Bojador south, and the whole southern part of that continent, was unknown or only

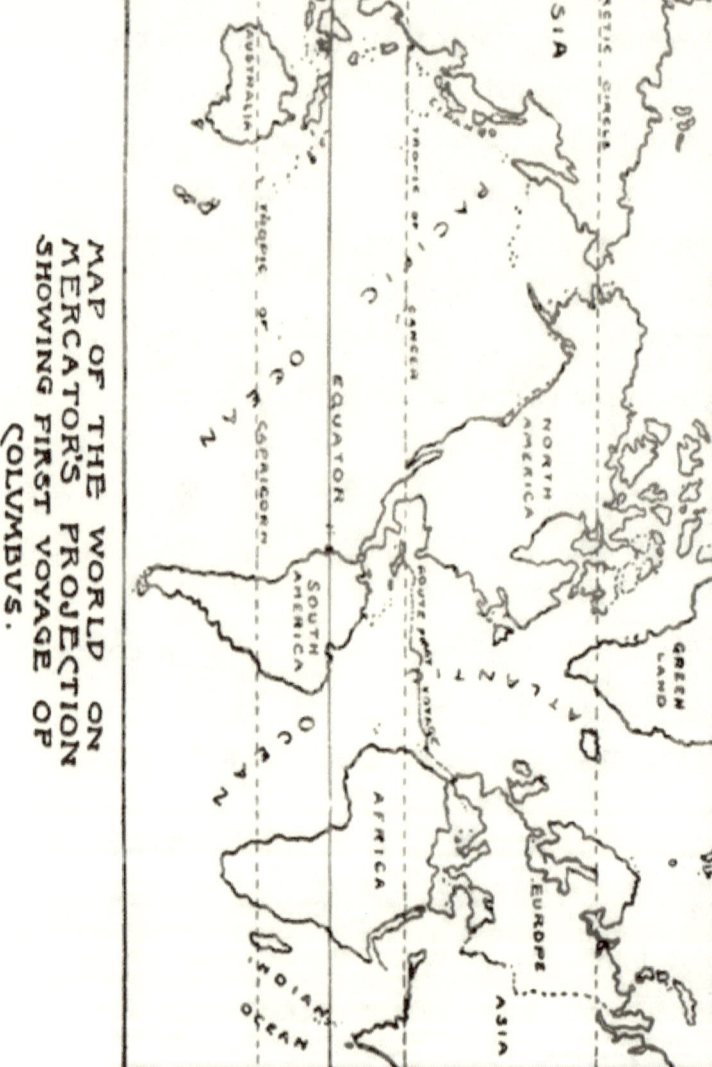

MAP OF THE WORLD ON MERCATOR'S PROJECTION SHOWING FIRST VOYAGE OF COLUMBUS.

conjectured, and that he supposed Asia and Africa were connected by land at the south. Southern Europe, Western Asia and Northern Africa were the only land regions tolerably well known to him; while as to Northern Europe, Eastern and Northern Asia and Southern Africa his work was pure conjecture. Of course he had no knowledge of the breadth of the Atlantic Ocean; and as for the great Pacific Ocean and its islands, and the continent we inhabit, he never knew of or suspected their existence.

If any one will construct a globe or make a map of the earth, leaving out the continent of America and the Pacific Ocean, they will have an approximate idea of the geography of Ptolemy. And we beg to bear in mind that this was about the length and breadth of the geographical knowledge possessed by Columbus when he sailed from Spain in 1492 to reach Asia by a short westerly voyage. So much then was the geographical knowledge of four hundred years ago. The fortunate, but nevertheless monstrous, error which Toscanelli and Columbus imbibed from Marinus and Ptolemy is now easily understood.

But also as favoring the project of Columbus, he had learned from Toscanelli, a fact unknown to Marinus or Ptolemy, to wit: that a large island was situated some distance off the east coast of China called by him Cipango or Zipangu. All together, this led Columbus to believe would reduce the real interval between the Canary Islands and lands off the east coast of China to three or four thousand miles.

CHAPTER VIII.

FROM the age of Thales to Ptolemy, some seven hundred and fifty years, astronomy, mathematics and geography had made great progress, and the problem of the earth's surface was gradually unfolding. But the early centuries of our era were doomed to intellectual blight and commercial stagnation. The clashings and contests between the old and new religions, extending to bloody contentions for empire as well, delayed the progress and development of art, science and commerce, so that at the end of a thousand years the material interests and intellectual status of Europe had retrograded rather than progressed. From the age of Ptolemy for a thousand years neither Egypt, Greece, Rome or Christendom produced a man whose additions to the fund of astronomical or geographical knowledge is worthy of mention as a contribution to the new intellectual life developed in the thirteenth, fourteenth and fifteenth centuries. Those dark and unhappy centuries, from the third to the thirteenth, put Columbus under no obligations for services rendered or theories advanced to aid him in solving the problem of a successful western voyage over the Atlantic.

Before the time of Columbus the mariner's compass was in use, as also the astrolabe and cross-staff—the two latter, rude instruments for determining positions at sea. The Canary, Madeira and Azores Islands had been discovered, and the art of printing had been recently introduced in Europe. When the Turks, in 1453, closed the caravan route to the east by way of Constantinople, Christian Europe began to feel the necessity of opening some new route for commerce and trade with the eastern countries.

Marco Polo, a Venetian gentleman, in 1295, returned from a prolonged visit through Persia, India and China. His descriptions of the magnificence, wealth and splendor, manufactures and productions of the extreme east, so far surpassing anything known in Europe, in gold gems, silks, spices and perfumes, that enraptured fancy pictured it as Elysium, El-

Dorado, the earthly paradise, the ever receding vision, the first and last happy dream of every age and clime. Marco Polo's father and uncle had been to China before, and were the first Europeans to visit that distant country. Kublai, King of China, made them his embassadors to the Pope, requesting His Holiness to send him one hundred learned men to teach his people Christianity, and instruct them in the arts and civilization of Europe.

On their second visit to China they took with them Marco, a young man then about twenty years of age, who was at once engaged in the service of the King, visiting all parts of the kingdom. He was evidently a keen observer, and after several years of governmental service the King much regretted to permit him to return to Europe. After his return to Venice he was taken prisoner in a war between Venice and Genoa. While detained as a prisoner of war at Genoa, a fellow prisoner wrote down at his dictation the story of his travels and adventures and all the wonderful things he had seen in the region of the extreme east. The second part of his book is descriptive of the different states and provinces of Asia, with notices of their wonderful sights and products, their curious customs and manners and remarkable events, and especially regarding the Emperor, Kublai, his riches, power, his court, wars and administration. The existence of the island of Japan, situated off the east coast of China, was first known by Toscanelli from the work of Marco Polo. Toscanelli communicated this fact to Columbus in 1474. The manuscript was later translated into several languages, and some eighty manuscript copies are still in existence.

As Columbus afterward ranked as the prince of navigators, so as truly was Marco Polo to that day the greatest traveler by land the world had produced. The wonders of Asia were thus brought vividly to the knowledge of Europeans. Italy may well boast this contribution to Europe, as well as the contributions of her other son, the courageous maritime hero, Christopher Columbus, who garnered the secrets of the dark Atlantic.

Nearly two hundred years had expired, however, before a real attempt was made to utilize the fund of information furnished by Marco Polo. At that day the art of printing had not been introduced in Europe, and that "traveling school house" or universal educator, the "newspaper," was yet a thing of the dim future. To-day the harnessed lightning would hasten to convey such a revelation, and before our old earth could perform one revolution or somersault, millions of people, to the remotest parts of the earth, would have read the strange and welcome news. Slow it was, but as the story of Marco Polo became gradually known and digested, it soon became the prime object of the nations of western Europe to reach the opulent and distant countries he had visited and described. Nor was an overland journey, requiring years to perform, practicable for the purposes and necessities of profitable and successful trade and commerce. Besides, the Turks then possessed the keys to the gates of the pathway. If there could be found an open sea-way around the south of Africa it would open a route by water, for the east coast of Africa as far south as Zanzibar was already known, and the crossing of the Indian Ocean would bring the navigator to the coveted prize. To this undertaking the Portuguese bent all their energies. To reach India and Asia by a continued and unbroken navigation was the crowning ambition of the time, for as yet a western voyage across the Atlantic was unsuggested.

The millennium of mental darkness was drawing to a close. The thousand years of bigotry, ignorance and superstition were amply fulfilled. The dawn of a more happy era is manifest, and the heralds are announcing the second birth of science, while mankind seem impelled by new and more reasonable impulses. The advent of great men is foreshadowed and the grand secrets of the earth are the coming revelation, while quickening, generous (though tardy) nature is about to bring forth the man to hasten the grand event, whose daring genius shall pierce the gloom of that long, dark night of ages, and lay open to mankind the boundless resources of a new world.

CHAPTER IX.

CHRISTOPHER COLUMBUS was born in Genoa, Italy, possibly as early as 1436, but as now seems more probable about 1446. The events of his early life are involved in much obscurity. Could what he in after years accomplished have been foreseen, every act of his early life would have been recorded to the minutest particular. He did not become an object attracting any observation or notoriety before we find him in correspondence with Paolo Toscanelli, in 1474, in reference to the feasibility of a westerly voyage to China and India. From that time until the 5th of May, 1487, it is impossible to place an exact date to any event in the life of Columbus. Neither to his first arrival in Portugal, his marriage, or the birth of his son Diego, the death of his wife, his conference with King John, or his leaving Portugal and his arrival in Spain, can exact dates be assigned.

We are informed that he left the University of Pavia at the age of fourteen years. Exactly how long he had been at the University we are not informed, but we are told that under the tutelage of Antonio da Terzega and Stefano di Faenza he studied astronomy, mathematics and navigation. These studies show us the natural tendency of his youthful mind, because they were a necessary preliminary to his future profession. His age, however, precludes the idea that he had become a proficient or profound scholar. Upon leaving the University it has generally been assumed that he immediately adopted the life of a seaman. Recent investigations, however, render such an assumption quite improbable.

Of his apprenticeship in navigation we possess no record. Therefore, as we find him mentioned as a resident of Genoa until 1470, or possibly 1473, and after that time in Portugal, there is a blank of ten years from his age, fourteen years in 1460 to 1470 or 1473, which we cannot fill up with events of his life with any certain or satisfactory data. In after years Columbus says of himself: "Wherever ship has sailed there have I journeyed." We know he visited the Greek Isles, the Guinea coast, England, and possibly Iceland, or more probably some other northern island. The earlier story of his being on a wrecked expedition, under an old corsair, and cast upon the coast of Portugal, must now be discredited. We can locate him in Portugal about 1470, certainly during 1473.

During his residence of some twelve or fourteen years in Portugal, we learn that he was married, and that his son, Diego, by that marriage was born to him. His wife had relatives among the navigators of the day, and from the logs of those veteran seamen he is said to have derived useful and interesting information. Part of his time was spent in Porto Santo, an island of the Madeira group, where he went with his wife to enjoy some property left her by her father. It was during this Portuguese sojourn that he busied himself in studying the works of Nearchus, Aristotle, Pliny, Roger Bacon, the cosmography of Cardinal Aliaco, the travels of Marco Polo and Mandeville, and the geography of Marinus and Ptolemy. His studies seem to bear relation exclusively to the sciences essential to his chosen profession, and are indicative of what he afterwards was to attempt to accomplish. It would be a pleasure to know just when and from what data he arrived at the conclusion that he could reach the east coast of Asia by a voyage westward from Europe. Part of his time was spent in making maps and charts for a livelihood, for he was a skillful draughtsman. It was a time when the air was filled with tales and propositions of discovery. The captains of Prince Henry, of Portugal, had been gradually pushing their voyages down the West African coasts, and in some of these voyages Columbus was a participant.

As early as 1474 he appears to have been in correspondence with Paolo Toscanelli, of Italy, a celebrated physician, astronomer and cosmographer, concerning the feasibility of a western voyage to Asia. Toscanelli was a philosopher and Columbus a courageous seaman. As to the possibilities of the proposed voyage, these men were of one mind and conclusion. Toscanelli seems to have been the first scholar and cosmographer to give Columbus emphatic encouragement to the undertaking.

It is said that Aristotle, Strabo and Seneca thought it might be possible to sail west to India. All that, if true, goes for next to nothing, as no suggestion was made as to its feasibility, and those authorities made no proposition of any attempt to prove or substantiate the theory.

In Columbus we find the very first man of our race (so far as we may know) who was deliberately preparing to make the definite voyage by the unknown westerly route to the easterly shores of Asia, thus completing a full knowledge of the circumference of the globe east and west. As to this project the world furnished him no competitor. Whoever has since crossed the Atlantic Ocean is under some obligation to him for performing his first voyage.

His accidental discovery of America we concede. We also concede his failure to sail to Asia. But we say once for all time that any possible previous undetermined and unpremeditated voyages to this continent, whereof is no chart and doubtful record, must count for nothing in the absence of marks and monuments of either colonization, conquest or possession.

As before stated, in formulating their philosophy, neither Toscanelli nor Columbus appear to have been controlled or influenced by the computed circumference of the earth by Eratosthenes, and both seem to have embraced the error of Marinus as to the enormous easterly extension of the Asiatic continent. Columbus, even as late as his third voyage, said: "The earth is much smaller than most people suppose;" but he does not say how large it is nor how large he thought it to be. Had he believed that the voyage from Europe by the west to Asia would cover 14,490 miles, we cannot readily believe he would have either contemplated or hazarded the experiment of navigating that expanse of unknown, dreaded and untraveled sea with three little boats and a mutinous crew.

At this point, while we observe Columbus maturing his plan and project for his western voyage of discovery, or rather his voyage to Asia, it is deemed appropriate to direct attention to the data from which he constructed his theories. Of course, it must be apparent to all that to plan his first voyage—nay!

more, before such an enterprise could find lodgment in human conception—at least two theories must be conceived and developed to their utmost limit as theories.

The first, relates to the form or sphericity of the earth; the second, to its size or circumference. The first, Columbus seems to have accepted as a fact proved. As to the second (its circumference), it is difficult, or rather impossible, to say just what his opinions were upon that matter. By taking such opinions as he has left us we obtain curious results. He sailed his first voyage in full confidence of reaching the east coast of Asia or the adjacent islands after sailing about 3000 miles. Taking the miles of a degree of longitude on the twenty-fifth degree of north latitude as sixty-three, and the distance around the earth on that parallel of latitude as 22,680 miles, and the true distance across Europe and Asia as 8190 miles, then to reach Asia by sailing west he must sail 14,490 miles. If he accepted Ptolemy that Europe and Asia extended over 180 degrees, then he must sail 11,340 miles. If he accepted Marinus, that Europe and Asia extended 225 degrees, then he must sail 7505 miles to reach the Asiatic coast. As he sailed 3500 miles west, that would still leave an interval of 4000 miles. If, however, he gathered the idea from Marco Polo that Cipango, or Japan, lay three or four thousand miles off the Asiatic coast, because he simply said that it was a great distance, then Columbus was justified in expecting to find Japan, or Cipango, about where he found San Domingo. In other words, by embracing the error of Marinus, and mistaking the distance that Japan lay off the Asiatic coast by some 3500 miles, made altogether a shortening of the earth's circumference upon latitude 25 degrees north of about 10,000 miles, a little more or less. Exactly how much or how little he really knew about these distances is very uncertain and indefinite. We are just about as likely to do him injustice by supposing he knew more than he did, as by assuming that he knew less than he might have known.

Events, however, crowded our hero forward, and he must have felt that no time was to be lost—for Portugal was on the alert, and had determined to reach India by circumnavigating Africa, if that were possible.

The competing spirit of maritime enterprise was fairly awakened, and the very air was full of rumored adventure, while the weird imaginings of many generations of medieval navigators began to assume quite tangible shape and substance. Nothing that had any bearing to fortify Columbus in his theory seems to have escaped his careful attention. Prolonged westerly gales had thrown upon the coasts pieces of wood and canes unknown in Europe, and the bodies of two men had come ashore at Flores, differing from Europeans. Perchance there might float before excited fancy the legendary islands of St. Brandan and the lost island of the Seven Cities.

At what particular time Columbus had definitely determined to undertake the westerly voyage we cannot determine, but most probably before the year 1484. Columbus was poor, without friends of means or influence to secure him an outfit, nor could the proposed expedition be wisely undertaken by an individual. There are reasons for believing that like a true son of

Italy he proposed the enterprise first to the Senate of Genoa. We are told that the project was rejected as visionary and impossible. He next offered the scheme to King John II, of Portugal. This appears to have been between 1482 and 1485, the probabilities indicating the latter date.

Accustomed as we are to our democratic manners and customs, and the ease with which our public functionaries are approached on all proper occasions, and for proper purposes by the humblest citizen, we must, to appreciate the difficulties and embarrassments that beset Columbus in Portugal, and afterwards in Spain, bring before our minds the fact that a mere citizen, simply, could make no direct approach to the sovereign, and no audience would be granted. A king or queen, by the grace of God, is one thing; a president or governor, elected by the people, is quite another thing. An officer elected for a short term by the people, and who generally desires a second term, is not generally known to be uncivil to the VOTER, by the grace of God and by virtue of the constitution. In those days it was quite an awful thing to be permitted to look upon the sovereign, while to speak in his presence would be audacious.

Without money, without possessing any voucher of learning from some university, without friends of influence, it mattered little that Columbus wished to present a scheme to result in the revolution of the moral and mental world—to give to Portugal, Spain or Europe more than the one-half of the surface of the globe. His scheme was too great and premature to command attention. In fact, it was looked upon by the learned as visionary, impracticable, impossible, and he was regarded as quite a lunatic. His claim, therefore, upon the attention of the royal ear was decidedly flimsy and uncertain. We are not definitely informed as to his gaining royal recognition from King John II, of Portugal. However, Columbus did lay his proposition, possibly, before the King in person. He wished to be furnished with a proper outfit, and proposed to reach Asia by sailing to the west. His demands for compensation, if successful, were substantially the same as will presently appear when his proposition was laid before the Spanish monarchs.

Notwithstanding the Portuguese had already determined to reach Asia by quite a different route from the one proposed by Columbus, yet King John appeared to appreciate the grand possibilities of the new scheme of Columbus, and to perceive somewhat the force of the argument by which he advocated his novel idea. Therefore, after a careful examination of the matter, the King referred the plan of Columbus to his council for geographic affairs. The report of the council was adverse to the undertaking. The Bishop of Ceuta, however, was so impressed by Columbus that, notwithstanding the adverse report of the council, he persuaded the King (who also favored the project) to carry out the scheme of Columbus without his knowledge, by sending out secretly a caravel on the mission. The caravel put to sea, but did not sail very far before the sailors lost all courage and compelled a retreat and return.

Of course, Columbus soon learned of this dishonorable attempt to appropriate his idea and scheme, and hastily and somewhat secretly left Portugal in disgust. Some thought he left thus clandestinely to avoid the

King, while others said it was to escape his creditors. The latter reason appears the more probable, as we gather from the fact that seven or eight years later King John wrote him a friendly letter, earnestly requesting him to return and engage in the service of Portugal, promising him immunity from trouble or annoyance from any civil or criminal process. This was, however, after he was committed to the service of Spain, and the offer was not accepted.

CHAPTER X.

ON leaving Portugal, Columbus probably went directly to Spain, still seeking a patron for his enterprise. Some authorities will have it that this is the period when he laid his scheme before the Senate of Genoa. The accounts of his plans and movements for the next few years are too conflicting to make it possible for us to feel certain that we have any orderly and historically authentic rendering, nor does it now matter that such is the case. Our conclusions will be the same, though our curiosity must remain ungratified. The more popular story is that Columbus, with his young son, stopped at the convent of La Rabida, near Palos, and making a rather abrupt acquaintance with the good old friar, Juan Perez de Marchena, so impressed him as he unbosomed his grand scheme that he received from him a letter to Ferdinand de Talevera, the Queen's confessor, designed to introduce him to the notice of the Court.

It seems very doubtful if he made such rapid progress toward the Spanish sovereigns, or that he on this first visit to Marchena really received a letter intended as an introduction to Court. It may well be doubted if Columbus, an entire stranger in Spain, was laboring under the delusion that his strange scheme would be as likely to command the approval of the Court, as to send him to a mad-house. His own good sense would dictate a slower and more cautious procedure. If he could impress his theory upon cosmographers or navigators, or some prince to whom he could more easily find access, he would secure recommendations that would put him on the highway to the Court, and secure him a patient even if also a prejudiced audience. He well knew how unpopular was his theory. His proposition was as novel, and at that time as seemingly preposterous, as would now seem a proposition to visit and explore that half of the moon whose face is never shown to mortal eyes.

The histories are quite unanimous in showing Columbus several years later (autumn of 1491) at La Rabida, when Friar Marchena wrote a friendly and potent letter in the interest of Columbus to Queen Isabella. He was undoubtedly at La Rabida on two occasions, and certainly found a friend in Juan Perez de Marchena; but the accounts of the transactions at these two visits have become intermixed by the historians. It seems more probable that Columbus made his proposition to the Duke of Medini Sidonia and the Duke of Medini Celi before he went to Cordova, where the matter of his proposed voyage was first laid before the sovereigns. The Duke of Medini Sidonia at first was favorably impressed with the project, but finally dropped into the popular error that the project was visionary.

The Duke of Medini Celi was a man of wealth and enterprise, and took an intelligent interest in the scheme of Columbus, and seriously thought of furnishing the necessary fleet. He entertained Columbus for quite a period (Navarrete thinks for nearly two years), but finally and wisely concluded the enterprise too vast for a subject to undertake. Conquest was to follow discovery, while trade, barter and piracy were closely related. Undoubtedly, as the actual facts disclosed after the discovery of the new lands, it needed the strong military power of a national authority to subdue and hold in subjection the lands discovered.

At this juncture Columbus had concluded to go to France and seek government aid, but was persuaded by his friend, the Duke (who seems to have fairly appreciated and approved his plan), to apply at once to the Spanish Court, and he gave him a friendly letter to the Queen. Upon the strength of this letter the Queen summoned Columbus to Court at Cordova. It is of little consequence to us whether Columbus reached the Spanish Court through the letter of Juan Perez de Marchena, or rather of the Duke of Medini Celi, or that he had letters first or last from both sources. We are pleased to know that in either or both cases he found a warm and intelligent as well as influential friend.

It appears to have been in the latter part of the year 1486 that Columbus reached Cordova, where the Spanish Court then was. It was an unpropitious time for Columbus. The war for the expulsion of the Moors was the engrossing business of the time, and both Ferdinand and Isabella followed the camp in person, while the stubborn resistance of the Moors kept them too busy to devote either time or attention to the proposition of Columbus. The sovereigns, through Talevera, probably were apprised of the arrival of Columbus and the nature of his business. It is not probable, however, that at this time Columbus was given an audience in person at Court. Columbus met Alonzo de Quintanella and made him a convert to his theory, and on the removal of the Court to Salamanca, Columbus was introduced to Archbishop Mendoza, sometimes called the third King of Spain. The Archbishop was converted to the project of Columbus, but at first thought it smacked strongly of heteradoxy; yet it was through his influence Columbus obtained a personal interview with the King. The result was that the sovereigns, being constantly engaged in the war, were unable to give much attention to the scheme; but, being enough impressed with it to desire holding Columbus partially committed to them, referred the whole matter to Ferdinand de Talevera, with directions to entertain Columbus at government expense. The date of May 5th, 1487, heretofore mentioned, contains an entry by the treasurer of the Catholic sovereigns as follows: "Given this day, three thousand maravedis [about eighteen dollars] to Christobal Colon, a stranger."

In 1487, Talevera summoned a court or junta of geographers and astronomers to confer with Columbus and obtain his plans and the arguments in their support, with directions to report to the sovereigns upon the feasibility and advisability of the proposed undertaking and expedition. In all governments and in all times this mode of investigation for the advice and information of the executive government is both proper and common. The junta selected in this case was a bad one for the interests of Columbus. Selected by our standard as to whether or not the individual members had already formed or expressed an opinion for or against the matter, we may assume that most of them would have been "challenged," or at least directed to "stand aside for the present." The jurors were mainly ecclesiastics—authorities, such as may be, in matters of faith. They seem to have required

COLUMBUS BEFORE THE JUNTA.

Columbus to prove his theory from the Bible and the writings of the fathers, for from these authorities they deluged him with texts and quotations to overthrow his theories. It would be more amusing than instructive to quote the various and ridiculous objections of those jurors, and at this day not especially interesting to note the logical arguments of Columbus, now so well known and understood by the merest school-boy. However, this distinguished jury was out a long time, and modern usage would have discharged it for disagreement at the end of two years or sooner. But it took the jurors three years and more to reach an agreement. And at last, in 1490 or 1491, they made a report unfavorable to Columbus and his project. Under these circumstances, as a matter of course, this unfavorable report, from what was thought the best authorities, almost of necessity prejudiced their Majesties against the undertaking of the proposed expedition. Columbus was now quite in despair, and appears to have resolved to proceed to France for the purpose of laying his proposition before the French King. Some authorities think that it was at this juncture that he sent his brother Bartholomew to England to submit his project to King Henry VII. It may, however, have been before this time; but at any rate nothing came of it. This procrastination and delay of the Court of Spain must have been exasperating to Columbus. On his journey to France he stopped at the convent of La Rabida to see his son and his good friend, Perez de Marchena. The time of this second visit to the convent of La Rabida must have been in the autumn of 1491, for it was in December of the same year that the Queen summoned Columbus from La Rabida to appear at Court at Santa Fe. We cannot agree with some of the historians who claim that it was at this period that Columbus was spending nearly two years with the Duke of Medini Celi. The time at his disposal would not permit it, nor does it appear reasonable that Columbus applied to the Dukes of Sidonia and Celi for an equipment for his voyage after the undertaking had been condemned by the learned junta and rejected by the sovereigns. The good old friar, Marchena, was in distress for Columbus, and at once sent for his neighbors, Dr. Garcia

Fernandez and **Martin Alonzo** Pinzon. An earnest and hasty conversation followed. A letter was prepared for Queen Isabella, and was sent by one Sebastian Rodriguez. The Queen was then at Santa Fe. He found ready access to her Majesty, and delivered the letter. Isabella wrote a letter replying to Juan Perez de Marchena, requesting him to come immediately to her Court, and directing him to retain Columbus—to await with hope her further pleasure.

On receiving this letter, the old friar mounted his mule and rode in haste to Court. He was promptly ushered to the royal presence, and we may rest assured the project of Columbus found in him an enthusiastic, powerful and potent advocate. The Queen was convinced, and requested that Columbus should be immediately forwarded to Court, sending him at the same time a purse of $216.00 to enable him to appear fairly presentable. Columbus found the Court at Granada, and arrived in time to witness the surrender of that place, which ended the Moorish war. This appears to have been in January, 1492. The sovereigns had all along named that event as the time when they would *personally* consider the proposal of Columbus, and they kept their word. Persons in their confidence were appointed to complete the negotiations with Columbus. It is here that he appears at his best. He felt such complete confidence in his project, that he demanded terms thought to be too exorbitant. He demanded for himself, and for his heirs in perpetuity, to be admiral of all seas traversed, viceroy of all lands discovered, and a tenth of all profits obtained by barter, conquest or otherwise.

These terms were not conceded, and the negotiations terminated. His terms now appear to have been rather extravagant, and undoubtedly were so considered even then. A prudent monarch might reasonably hesitate to grant so much. Columbus, however, proposed no compromise or second price for his services. Again he actually set out on his journey to France. There must have been consternation at the Spanish Court, and a hurried consultation between those who favored the scheme of Columbus. Luis de St. Angel, receiver of the ecclesiastical revenues of the crown of Aragon, was put forth as their spokesman, to make another effort to secure the services of Columbus, for *he* was now evidently master of the situation. He appears no longer a pauper supplicant, but is going to make at least one-half of the bargain. In fact, he alone dictated the terms, and the sovereigns accepted them. Yes, his terms will be granted (reluctantly by Ferdinand); but the terms will eventually prove to be the beginning of his downfall, and result in his final disgrace and degradation. St. Angel must have pressed the proposition of Columbus forcibly upon Isabella, for she suddenly declared for the expedition, saying she would undertake it for her own crown of Castile; and if great haste were necessary, she would pledge her crown jewels to meet the expenses. St. Angel told her it would not be necessary. Bless her memory! for when a woman will pledge her jewels or jewelry, she means business. So rapidly did these events transpire that Columbus was overtaken when only six miles from Santa Fe, whither he returned, and where, on the 17th day of April, 1492, the final agreement between himself and the sovereigns was duly signed and sealed. The original terms of

Columbus were so modified that he might then, and at all times, contribute one-eighth of the expense and receive one-eighth of the profits. The original terms as to his offices and titles were granted as at first demanded.

The success of winning the QUEEN, and through her the KING, to the scheme of Columbus, is undoubtedly due to the timely and potent influences of Juan Perez de Marchena, Alexander Geraldinus, Archbishop Mendoza, Diego de Deza, the Duke of Medini Celi, Quintanelli and St. Angel—the two latter Ministers of Finance. From all the historians of the time and events, we gather the opinion that Ferdinand would scarcely have patronized the novel undertaking without the impelling influence of Isabella. The King was slow, cautious, calculating and cold. These are the conventional terms quite universally applied to King Ferdinand; but a more liberal expression, and probably more exact, would be, that he looked upon the project as a matter of business, to be entered into and executed upon business principles.

Isabella was Queen in her own right; and if, like

Ferdinand, the approach to the reason and intellect was difficult, yet the avenues to her heart in the cause of humanity, and bringing to the true faith (as she understood it) millions of the heathen world, were easily traversed. It is supposable that King Ferdinand, Mendoza, Quintanelli, Marchena and St. Angel had quite as good ideas of the costs and uncertainties of the expedition, as well as the possible commercial and financial advantages that might result from the scheme of Columbus, as had the Queen. Yet it was by a different line of argument that she was made a convert than that which operated upon them. Certainly no woman, before or since, has enjoyed the high distinction and honor of signing an agreement so momentous in results. In our admiration for the great navigator, let us not be unmindful of the signal good offices rendered in this behalf by this queenly woman and womanly Queen. Columbus was a devout churchman, and declared his purpose to reach Cipango and Cathay, and to convert the Grand Khan to the Christian faith. He expressed the determination to devote his prospective gains or profits to the raising and equipping a crusading army of four thousand horse and fifty thousand foot, for the retaking of the Holy Sepulchre at Jerusalem.

By a memorandum, which is here inserted, it appears the sovereigns felt a commendable anxiety to make a favorable impression upon the potentate near the rising sun. This little memorandum also shows unmistakably that the sovereigns, as well as Columbus, had in mind as the objective point of the expedition the eastern coast of Asia, and not any intermediate or unknown land. They therefore furnished Columbus with the following unique letter of introduction to the supposed eastern sovereign:

"FERDINAND AND ISABELLA TO KING ———.

"The sovereigns have heard that he and his subjects entertain great love for them and for Spain. They are, moreover, informed that he and his subjects very much wish to hear news from Spain, and send their Admiral, Ch. Columbus, who will tell them that they are in good health and perfect prosperity. Granada, April 30th, 1492."

About two hundred years before this date (1295, the date of the return of Marco Polo from Cathay) there might possibly have been some sense, propriety, point or appropriateness in inditing such a letter. It is quite apparent that the King and Queen had in their minds King Kublai, so grandly described by Marco Polo. As the sovereigns did not know and had no means of knowing who, or if any one, then occupied the throne of Kublai, or, if so, who might be his successor, it appears that their statement: "That they had heard that he and his subjects entertained great love for them and for Spain, and that they are informed that he and his subjects very much desire to hear news from Spain," was a very late reply to an entirely imaginary inquiry, and a strange apology for their somewhat presumptuous and preposterous letter.

It is not apparent how Columbus could have met his one-eighth of the expense, except that his good friend, Juan Perez de Marchena, induced Martin Alonzo and Vincente Yanez Pinzon to subscribe his share.

Three small vessels were to be fitted out: the Santa Maria, a decked ship, with a crew of fifty men, the Admiral Columbus in command; the Pinta, thirty men, commanded by Martin Alonzo Pinzon; and the

Nina, twenty-four men, commanded by Vincente Yanez Pinzon—the two latter were caravels without decks.

FLEET OF COLUMBUS.

The real number of men who embarked on the expedition is uncertain. The estimates range between one hundred and one hundred and thirty men. Our ordinary idea of ships requires some modification to appreciate such small craft as ocean rangers. The largest vessel was from fifty to seventy feet in length, and twenty feet beam—a sort of elongated tub.

Never again in this world will such a fleet plow the ocean waves upon an errand so momentous in results. So fearful were the men of the dangerous character of the expedition that indemnity to criminals was offered to fill the quota of men. When all was ready to sail, the friends of the crews gave up all hope of ever seeing them again, and wept and mourned as for friends who would never return. Before lifting anchor, Columbus and his men, as was always his custom in each new adventure, proceeded to the church and partook of the Holy Sacrament.

As we glance back at the narration of events, the variance of any one of which might have defeated the grand discovery of Columbus, we may better understand his frequently-expressed opinion: "That he was but a humble instrument, guided by the inspiration of Providence, to bring together the ends of the earth" (to connect a knowledge of the unknown with the known). However, we may be permitted to discover, in the ten thousand miles which yet separated the lands he discovered from Asia, that he had mistaken or misinterpreted the Divine will and intention. Yet

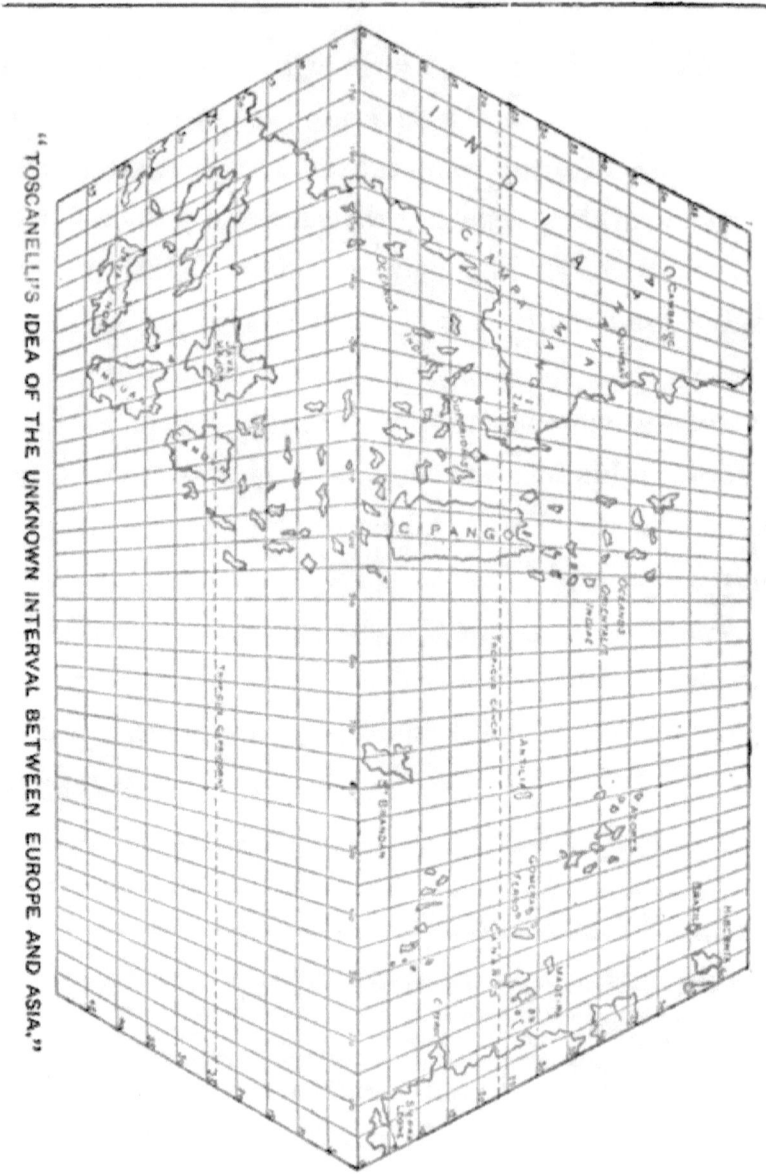

"TOSCANELLI'S IDEA OF THE UNKNOWN INTERVAL BETWEEN EUROPE AND ASIA."

undoubtedly his discoveries had both a direct and indirect tendency to hasten the full and final revelation of the whole circumference of the earth.

The expedition was then in readiness to proceed upon its novel and uncertain voyage. Before hoisting sail, however, this seems a proper place to enumerate some of the modern means, methods, instruments, etc., now used or known in aid of navigation, none of which were then known or used. The log, for measuring the velocity of sailing; the telescope; the position of the satellites of Jupiter; the dipping-needle; the watch or chronometer; a sea-chart of ocean currents, and sextant for determining latitude, and the reefing of sails. Of course he could have no sea-map, showing islands, rocks, shoals, or shores, except such as the fertile imagination of Toscanelli could invent. Such a chart he had, and by it his voyage was governed.

CHAPTER XI.

ON Friday, the 3d day of August, 1492, at eight o'clock in the morning, the ships sailed from the port of Palos and stood out for the Canary Islands, which Columbus and Toscanelli were right in supposing lay upon about the same parallel of latitude as Japan or Zipangu. On the third day out, the Pinta lost her rudder, and on the 9th of August the fleet put in at Teneriffe to refit the disabled caravel. Here they remained until the 6th of September, when learning, as is said, that a Portuguese fleet was in their pursuit, they again put to sea, sailing nearly due west. From the Canary Islands, where the trans-Atlantic voyage commenced, the average route of Columbus followed about upon the twenty-fifth parallel of north latitude, the length of a degree of longitude thereon being sixty-three miles and the earth's circumference on the same latitude 22,680 miles. A gentle breeze bore them along safely and without incident or accident at the average rate of

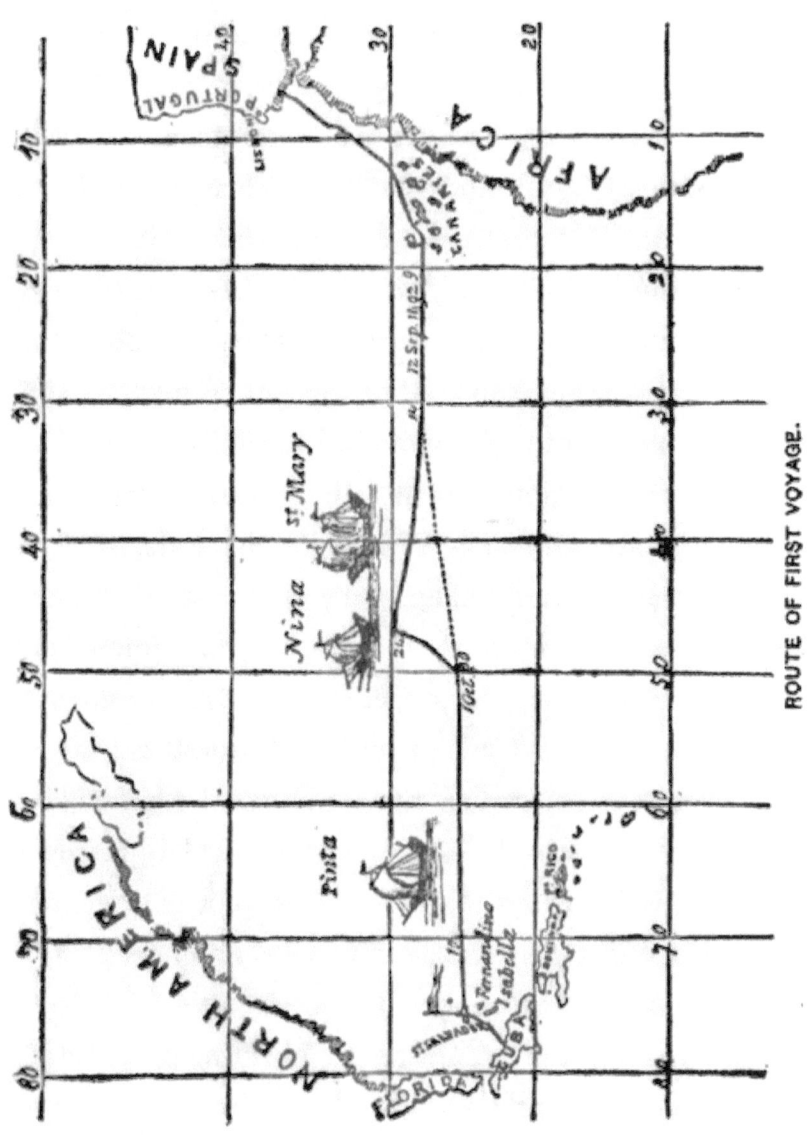

ROUTE OF FIRST VOYAGE.

about 100 miles per day of twenty-four hours. It has been said that the seamen were very much frightened by the variation of the magnetic needle, on the 13th of September, and that the explanation of the cause by the Admiral quieted their fears. This is as clear as mud; for the biggest land-lubber on the expedition must have known just as much about the cause as did the Admiral, or any other man to this day. On the 17th of September the crews began to be uneasy and clamorous to return. With the prevailing ignorance and superstitions of the time, we can readily imagine the feelings, arguments and dangers which the crews set forth as reason for an immediate turning around of the expedition and returning to Spain. It is not difficult for us to imagine the answers and assurances by which their commander attempted to allay their fears. There is a general agreement among the historians that Columbus kept two reckonings of the distance sailed—a true reckoning for himself, and a subtracted one to deceive his frightened crew. If, under the circumstances, this was pardonable, certainly the commanders of the other vessels, the pilots, or even the crews, could just as well and with just as much precision estimate the velocity of the ships and the distance sailed as the Admiral.

The statement of Oviedo, that Columbus at one time compromised with his frightened and mutinous crews, promising to return if land were not discovered in three days, is not probable or admitted by any modern historian. Still westward they sailed, borne along by gentle breezes, and on the 25th of September, and again on the 7th of October, there were false alarms of land. The signs of nearing land for the last two or three days of the voyage were assuring. On the evening of the 11th of October, a sharp lookout was ordered. At two o'clock on the morning of the 12th of October, Roderigo de Triana, a sailor on the Pinta, announced the sight of land, and an alarm gun was fired.

Columbus afterwards claimed that he had perceived a light ahead at eleven o'clock on the evening of the 11th, and secured a reward that had been promised by the sovereigns to the one who should first discover land.

At sunrise on the morning of the 12th a landing was made. Columbus, in full uniform, accompanied by the officers of the fleet and a portion of the sailors, and bearing the royal standard of Spain, took formal possession of the island for Spain, at the same time planting the royal standard and the emblem of the cross. The island discovered belonged to the Bahama group, and there is now some uncertainty as to the precise island of his landfall. The better opinion seems to designate " Watling's Island," as the Guanahani of the natives. The distinguished honor, however, has been claimed for four other islands in more or less close proximity. Columbus christened the island " San Salvador."

The great mission of Columbus was then substantially completed. He had accepted the challenge to all former navigators, and nature's defiance to all preceding ages; he had made a gallant fight, and now a well-earned victory came to reward his labors. The bugaboo of uncounted ages vanished before his conquering sails, and was thoroughly exterminated by the successful completion of the voyage of his three

LANDING OF COLUMBUS.

little boats. Henceforth and forever there will be no dark and dreadful Atlantic—no threatening and fearful western sea of darkness. Like magic, the fearful imaginary monsters, so seemingly real, and always just beyond the scope of sane vision, contracted to nothingness, and hereafter will exist only like the memories of a hideous dream of a disturbed sleep. Hereafter this great ocean road is to become the greatest and grandest route for profitable commerce and the most traveled route for pleasure and pleasant pastime on our globe. The safe and successful voyage of Columbus must have made the old sea-dogs of Europe fairly grin at their own ignorance and cowardice, and possibly to curse the event that forever closed the door to the high honor pertaining to a first successful navigation across the Atlantic.

The triumph of Columbus, as will presently be observed, from its very simplicity, was short lived, for as he afterwards, in 1498, wrote to the sovereigns: " Now that I have shown them the way, the very tailors want to become explorers." Of course, it may be said that Columbus had not yet discovered the main land of the American continent. That is so; but he had traversed the Atlantic waters and came upon solid land, beyond the alleged dreadful sea, some 3500 miles westward from his starting point. Sailing from thence to almost any point of the compass, except by a return upon his outward course, he or others must of necessity, and finally did, arrive upon the main land of both North and South America.

Columbus remained in the vicinity until January, 1493, meantime discovering Cuba, Hispaniola (afterwards Hayti, now known as San Domingo), and several other smaller islands. On the coast of Hispaniola his own vessel was wrecked, and out of her timbers a small fortress was erected at La Navidad, and forty-three men were left there to explore the island, collect gold, and await his return voyage from Spain. Having secured some specimens of gold, native curiosities, trinkets, native birds, animals, plants, gums, spices and other natural productions, he took on board nine of the natives and proceeded on his return voyage, arriving at the Azores February 18th, and the Port of Palos on the 15th of March, 1493.

CHAPTER XII.

THE Court was then at Barcelona. Columbus dispatched letters to the sovereigns announcing his arrival, the success of the expedition, and at once proceeded in person to lay before their Majesties, the world, and particularly before those who had so persistently opposed and ridiculed his theories, the evidences of his triumph. We may surmise that the miserable criminals, who mainly constituted his crews, experienced some of their commander's exultant feelings, and in consequential manner claimed some of the distinction pertaining to the first voyage, completing the supposed proof of the sphericity of the earth.

A voyage up the Mediterranean Sea to Barcelona would not bring before the people of the country with such notorious prominence the astonishing features and results of the trans-Atlantic voyage as the more leisurely journey by land, attended by rather pompous entries and transits into and through the villages along the line of the overland journey. Artemus Ward once asked, "What is the use of having jewelry unless you wear it?" Columbus determined to go by the overland route.

When Columbus formed his procession for the Court at Barcelona, enthusiam put on full head of steam. It took him about a month to make the journey. The Indies, as well as the Indians, had been found, as all believed. The rude golden trinkets were prominently exposed to the general view. Rare birds and animals, heretofore unknown and unseen by Europeans, were paraded in style. The productions of the strange land had their places assigned, while the natives were decked in their ludicrous gay trappings and feathery garb. Altogether it appeared so strange and unusual to behold these things from beyond the sea of darkness, that it is little wonder the streets were thronged, the air resounding with tumultuous, victorious shouts, and that the great discoverer appeared almost an object of worship and adoration.

But the climax was reached when the procession drew up in the presence of the sovereigns, and Columbus, in a triumphant but dignified manner, related the story of his voyage and discoveries. The sovereigns, dignitaries and all present fell upon their knees, giving thanks to God for the success of the expedition. The cathedral choir chanted the "Te-Deum Laudamus." The enemies of the Admiral, and all who had combated and ridiculed his theories, were silent, yea, dumb. Here before them all, and with what appeared abundant proofs, and witnesses, animate and inanimate, stood this great seaman and navigator, whom all conceded had sailed by the west to Asia and India, and safely returned. The sum total of the rumored wealth of India and Asia was ready to tumble into and repose in the lap of Spain.

It were well, were it possible, here to cut short our story and leave Columbus in the enjoyment of the honors he had so gallantly won. It is the privilege of romance and fiction to draw the curtain at the point or period where the hero might choose, leaving him to repose on the summit of his glory. Not so with history. History must relate the whole story, and may not close its narrative until every necessary fact and circumstance is duly recorded, regardless of the consequences to the name, fame or reputation of any one.

To cut the story of Columbus at this point, we would leave him temporarily outranking every human being in the whole world, excepting alone his sovereigns and the supreme head of the Church. He rode beside the King, and was a welcome guest of the highest dignitaries of the State and Church.

As Sebastian Cabot intimates, "a sort of divinity seemed for the time to overshadow him." Within seven short years his wine cup of joy will be filled with vinegar and gall, his name and fame become bywords, he will be shorne of his honors, his titles, his offices and his emoluments, and sink into almost entire insignificance. That uncertain thing, designated "Public Sentiment," or "Public Esteem," will swing to the opposite extreme and drop its one day hero to a beggar's estate. It is said "that time at last makes all things even," etc. The clarifying effects of four hundred years may not be sufficient to make the voyages or discoveries of Columbus appear to us superhuman or supernatural; but sober judgment will not permit us to cast entirely aside or to forget his great service to science, to commerce, and to humanity.

The people of this day and generation will do his name, fame and memory ample justice, and to the full extent of their ability publicly rectify the wrongs done to and endured by this great man at the hands of the people of his own day and generation.

Columbus was an enthusiast; his statements, generally careless, were often contradictory, and sometimes absurd, while his descriptions of prospective wealth were overdrawn and unwarranted. Hence, as the sequel will show, charges of deception and dishonesty were easily and apparently not without some foundation made against him. It became difficult and impossible for him to sustain the very expectations he had unwittingly excited. Years of hard labor in the new country were required to produce and cause to yield in its sugar, rum, cotton, tobacco, wheat, corn, fruits, pork and beef—its real, substantial and ever recurring wealth, rather than the gathering of a few scattered nuggets of gold, soon exhausted, with no second crop. The great discoverer was not entirely unlike his companions. Gold, gold! yellow gold! without money, labor or price, was the first and last thought, and all enormities and cruelties were justified in its acquisition.

At this point the native Indians may fairly claim at least a passing notice. When their island homes were first invaded by the Spaniards, their population may have been somewhere between one and three millions. They possessed their lands in fee, and occupied the same as tenants in common. They owed neither debts, service nor allegiance to any other people in the world. Their right, therefore, to their lands, property and liberty, was absolute, and as preciously sacred as those of any other people on the face of the earth. When the Spaniards made a descent upon them, they were but poorly prepared to resist the invasion or protect against encroachments upon their natural rights. They were without letters or learning, unclothed, and had no accumulations of personal property, had no substantial dwellings, and were unacquainted with the use of metals, had made no progress in agriculture, and had substantially no trade or commerce, living in a most primitive state, untouched by the breath of civilization, passing their days in apparently a happy ease and idleness.

They extended a generous welcome to their white brothers, acknowledging their own inferiority by every act and gesture, unwittingly kissing the hands that were soon to bind them in a slavery to which death were preferable. Their weapons of defence were bows and arrows, clubs and wooden spears. The Spaniards were protected by iron mail, had cannon, muskets, lances, swords, cross-bows, and supplemented their offensive equipment with blood-hounds. To make the Indian search and delve for gold, or till the soil for the invaders, the lash was unsparingly applied to their naked bodies, and if attempts were made to escape the murderous blood-hounds were put upon their track to hunt them out and tear them to pieces.

Such a state of slavery could not long endure or be endured. Death by the sword, death from the blood-hound, death from starvation, and, in their desperation, self-inflicted death. In a few short years the harvest of death was complete. The native islanders were entirely annihilated; the white men were victorious—they had come to stay. The slow torture of captives by fire, since practiced by native savages, was a refinement of cruelty first taught them by the white conquerors of the West Indies.

The polished apologies that have been made to screen from just indignation and contempt the perpetrators of the horrid atrocities in the subjugation and depopulation of the West Indies, by those who professed for their primary object the conversion of the natives to Christianity and the salvation of their souls, is as audacious and cowardly as it is hypocritical, false and abominable. The cruel, wicked, unnecessary and wanton destruction of the natives of the West Indies makes the blackest page in modern history. But, in passing judgment upon that act, it is not a pleasant duty to be obliged to admit that the process of native destruction there so horribly inaugurated, later generations in much less savage manner have nearly completed throughout the continental land. It is, therefore, not very wonderful that the natives have generally rejected a religion professed by their conquerors and exterminators.

It is from the romantic pen of Mr. Irving that the pompous description of the pageant and triumph at Barcelona is generally taken. To a judicious critic that performance ought not to have appeared quite so much like "Barnum's Greatest Show on Earth" to the country small boy. Bracelets, coronets, ornaments of gold and feathers upon the Indians, rare plants, live parrots and stuffed birds, while "great care was taken to make a conspicuous display of Indian coronets, bracelets and other decorations of gold which might give an idea of the wealth of the newly-discovered regions." All were happily deceived and pleased with the show. The critic's eye must have been closed during the circus. In the enthusiasm and excitement of the moment a temporary mental alienation seems to have pervaded, or at least there appears a decided absence of common sense. What was there to be seen in a live parrot, stuffed birds, and a few nuggets of native gold, unmanufactured, dangling about those native savages, or in some quills sticking about their heads, to indicate that they came from a region of boundless wealth? Nothing! The cause for this stupid frenzy and golden dream is not beyond our power to understand. The story of Marco Polo, just at this time, had a peculiar charm and became very interesting, although it had lain quite dormant for nearly two hundred years. The proposition of Columbus to sail by a short voyage to Asia, now that it had been accomplished, as was generally supposed, awakened this long slumber of indifference, to realize that the unbounded wealth of Asia was ready to be cropped by Spain. Nor does it look to us as if it were expected to be acquired by what we know as honest and honorable barter or trade—of buying and selling—but by a shorter and cheaper process than by paying dollars, each one of which represented a hard day's work. Columbus was undoubtedly mistaken as to where he had been; but, supposing he had reached Asia, he was anxious to support his claim that he was or had been on the confines of the regions of marvelous wealth which

Marco Polo had seen and described. He made his display look as much like it as was possible, and if he may have entertained any private doubts, not so with the people who witnessed his show. They reached the tempting conclusion by jumping all obstacles—for they saw, or thought they did, in this rude display, Asiatic kings, queens and princes, golden crowns, golden bracelets, golden rings, gold spectacles, gold pens, gold thimbles, gold watches, gold beads, gold-headed canes, bags of golden coin, golden slippers? crowns of sparkling diamonds, silken dresses, feather-trimmed bonnets, India shawls, and sniffed aromatic spices and loud perfumes.

"What came ye out to see?" Spain did not awaken from this vision—this auriferous dream—until reports came home from the gold-seekers and adventurers who rushed to the new land on the second expedition of Columbus. On reaching Hispaniola they found the colonists that had been left at La Navidad on the first voyage had all been killed, and their fortress reduced to ruin. There were no stores of food, no accumulation of property among the natives; and as for gold, there was none accumulated or to be obtained, except by the usual slow, painful, tedious and laborious methods. To many, the climate proved unhealthy; the gold-seekers became disheartened, discouraged and rebellious, and rashly and cruelly charged all their misfortunes upon Columbus.

The pageant of Barcelona at length could be interpreted and measured by the standards of common sense. The set-back was humiliating to Columbus and exasperating to the colonists. As the story proceeds we shall observe the triumph of Barcelona culminated in the return of Columbus from his third voyage a prisoner, loaded with iron chains instead of golden nuggets like his Indian captives at Barcelona.

The title of Viceroy proved his destruction. One might wish he had renounced the title and its burdens, and confined his labors to explorations. It is evident that the act or event which the world is now about to commemorate is limited to and focused upon the great discovery. Other honors either belong to, or must be shared with, other navigators and governors.

Columbus made three more voyages to what finally received the name of the "West Indies," in contradistinction to the "Indies" situated ten thousand miles further to the west.

These pages are not designed for a full biography of Columbus, or for a history of the early colonization or settlement of the "West India Islands" and continental America. As indicated in the Preface, we confine our story within the briefest limits possible to illustrate the significance of our approaching international commemoration of the "Discovery of America by Columbus." Yet perhaps it is desirable to place before the reader a synopsis of the various expeditions sent out to the West Indies, for the purpose of colonization, *previous to the death of Columbus.*

The first expedition of discovery is already noted.

The second expedition, consisting of seventeen ships, with fifteen hundred men, part of whom were in government employ and the remainder volunteers, sailed from Spain September 25th, 1493; Christopher Columbus in command as Admiral and Viceroy. From this voyage Columbus returned to Spain June 11th, 1496.

The third expedition consisted of six ships, with about five hundred men, with the privilege to take along thirty females. It does not appear that any females embarked. Columbus, in command of the expedition, sailed from Spain May 30th, 1498. Columbus returned to Spain in October or November, 1500, a prisoner in chains, suspended from all authority.

The fourth expedition, consisting of thirty ships, with about twenty-five hundred persons, among whom were seventy married men of distinction, accompanied by their wives and families, sailed from Spain February 13th, 1502, Don Nicholos de Ovando in command as Governor of the West India colonies, in place of Bobadilla, who suspended Columbus, and in the meantime had acted as Governor-General.

This last expedition was the first one which contained all the elements necessary for founding a successful and permanent colony. Never in the history of mankind has a colony been successfully organized or established without the peculiar and civilizing aid and influence of women, and their cheerful and comforting presence. We wonder why this important matter was neglected by all the former expeditions. Whether women alone could colonize with success, we will not stop to debate; men alone cannot.

It has already been mentioned that Columbus, on his third voyage, saw the South American continent, at the mouth of the river Orinoco, and that on his fourth voyage he coasted Honduras and Costa Rica, to the narrowest part of the Isthmus of Darien. It would be perhaps interesting to recount the story of his last voyages in full, but they in no great measure pertain to our subject. Suffice to say that they brought nothing but disaster, disappointment, vexation and trouble to Columbus. There was nothing in them to stay the rapidly declining fame and final downfall of the Admiral. The sun of his temporary glory was half eclipsed during his second voyage, and became entirely obscured at the termination of his third voyage.

Loud complaints and disparaging reports reached the royal ears in regard to the Admiral's administration of affairs at San Domingo, while on his second voyage. His waning standing at Court, instigated, (as he alleged) by his enemies, caused him to repair to Spain. Here he seemingly ingratiated himself with the sovereigns again, and his third expedition was determined upon.

There had been no difficulty experienced in getting an abundance of volunteers to go upon the second expedition, but the experience of the colonists was so different from what had been anticipated—so fruitless in accumulating wealth—that when the third expedition was being fitted out, there was great difficulty in finding volunteers, and resort was had to the methods of the first expedition, to wit, to induce criminals—those who were condemned to banishment or the galleys—to go, in lieu of enduring the pains and penalties pronounced against them for their crimes.

No sooner, however, did Columbus resume the administration of affairs at San Domingo than rebellions of the colonists began to hatch against him and defy his authority. The truth perhaps is, that his schooling and early discipline had not been of the kind to qualify him for a viceroy—a governor of men and a planter of colonies. True, he had obtained these high-sounding titles, but he quite certainly misunderstood their significance, and had but a limited and obscure idea of their just and proper functions. As before, so now, every vessel returning to Spain was freighted with evil reports and loud complaints against his government.

The sovereigns were deeply interested in the success of the colonies as well as Columbus, and they were kept well informed as to the conduct of affairs at San Domingo. It could therefore have been little less than disheartening when they learned that the revolt of Roldan and his followers had forced Columbus to compromise with and concede every humiliating demand made of him by those in rebellion against his authority. Some of the rebels were desirous of returning to Spain, and Roldan compelled Columbus to give these rebels certificates of good character to be shown for their protection when they should arrive in Spain. At the same time Columbus explained the true state of affairs to his sovereigns without the knowledge of the rebels. The sovereigns sent out a trusted officer (Don Francisco de Bobadilla), clothed with ample powers to make inquiries of the disorders, to ascertain who was in fault, to restore order, and if necessary to suspend from command whomsoever he would, and to send those in default prisoners to Spain.

It is unnecessary to inquire now, whether Bobadilla acted with due prudence, caution or wisdom; but he certainly did not exceed his powers or commission, though the sovereigns afterwards virtually said he did. He made Columbus and both his brothers prisoners and sent them in irons to Spain, together with his report of the reasons for such an apparently high-handed measure.

During the voyage homeward Columbus wrote a letter to Dona Juana de la Torre, a confidant of Queen Isabella, and the "aya" or nurse of Prince Juan, giving his statement of his own case and in his own way. Why did he not address his sovereigns? We may surmise he had an object in view. The sons of Columbus were pages to Prince Juan and Queen Isabella. Through the aid of the captain of the vessel on which Columbus was confined, he expressed this letter to its destination several days before the official report sent home by Bobadilla was forwarded to the King. We may feel assured that this pathetic letter of Columbus was shown to the *Queen* in haste. Queen Isabella was the best friend Columbus ever had. Columbus always seemed to be able to more favorably impress women than men. We may also surmise that it was his intention and design that this letter should be passed to the hands of Isabella before it should be possible for the King and the Cabinet to see the accusations against him contained in the report of Bobadilla.

As the sovereigns, until the receipt of that letter, had no intimation as to what Bobadilla had done, the news was somewhat shocking. It was not in human nature to calmly behold Columbus, now returned in irons from the supposed Indies, he had so recently discovered and presented to Spain. Orders were issued for his immediate release, and he was politely summoned to Court. On beholding him in his sorry plight, it is said that Queen Isabella was moved to tears. The sovereigns evidently tried to shirk responsibility for his arrest and degradation by alleging that Bobadilla had exceeded his authority, and promising to recall him, and made promises to restore Columbus to his command and to his titles. But it was never done, and most likely was not really intended. Such was the public reaction in favor of Columbus, that no public attention was paid to the charges against him. Bobadilla was recalled, but Ovando, and not Columbus, was sent out to take charge of the colonies.

Columbus, some time after this, was made commander of four small vessels, with 150 men, to make explorations for a fancied strait beyond the Gulf of Mexico, with special directions not to stop at San Domingo on his outward voyage.

The Queen died about the time that he returned from his fourth and last voyage. Columbus continued to press his claims to his titles and his emoluments upon King Ferdinand, but was never able to obtain any satisfaction for what he claimed to be his just rights and dues. He died, as before stated, at Valladolid, May 20th, 1506, poor, neglected, broken-hearted, unrestored to his titles or command, unwept and unsung. In this sad plight the Spanish nation has unjustly and ungenerously allowed the name, fame and memory of Columbus to remain: a mournful ending to a remarkable career.

The causes which led to and terminated in his downfall and disgrace, in so far as he contributed to the same, is pretty well indicated already. In addition to the causes mentioned, we beg to suggest some others, which operated to produce the unhappy result.

First, as to the King. He had sagaciously considered the original demands of Columbus exorbitant and the powers and prerogatives granted dangerous to confer even upon a subject, but more especially so upon a stranger and foreigner. He had hesitated to grant the demands of Columbus, but he was obliged to make the promise or forego the possibilities of the expedition. When, therefore, somewhat of the magnitude of the discoveries became known, he was undoubtedly quick to embrace the first opportunity or excuse upon which to terminate the agreement, and among other matters, to use the statements of the enemies of Columbus (fearing justly or otherwise), that there might a time come when Columbus would assume sovereignty, instead of being content with Vice-Royalty, of the new and distant lands. It is but charitable to conclude that the sovereigns on the return of Columbus from his third voyage, had become satisfied of the thorough inability or incompetence of Columbus to manage and govern the new colonies. Something must be done, for the demands and necessities of State are inexorable, and responsibility rests upon the sovereign power. The lesser power must yield to the greater. Columbus was sacrificed. The act was boldly performed, but it was not done without palliating circumstances (and apparently good), or what the sovereigns believed to be sufficient reasons.

The matter which was most likely to prejudice the Queen, was the undoubted cruelty which Columbus and his colonists practiced upon the simple-minded Indians, and his persistence in enslaving them, against the frequently expressed wishes of her majesty. Every line of history bespeaks the tender regard she had for the well-being and fair treatment she desired for these children of nature and of the forest. Among the instructions of the sovereigns to the second expedition, "the Admiral is ordered to labor in all possible ways to bring the dwellers in the Indies to a knowledge of the Holy Catholic faith, and that this may be done the more easily, all the armada is to be charged to deal lovingly with the Indians. The Admiral is to make them presents and to honor them much, and if by chance any person or persons should treat the Indians ill, in any manner whatever, the Admiral is to chastise such evil doers severely." Columbus sent home five shiploads of the natives at one time, to be sold in the markets of Seville as slaves. Queen Isabella in severe terms denounced the act and ordered them all returned to their country and friends.

As regards the average Spanish Hidalgo gold seeker and adventurer, he saw in Columbus an upstart and pretentious foreigner, exercising Vice-Royal authority over him in the new lands, and being disappointed and disgusted with his ill luck in accumulating gold, as if he expected golden nuggets to grow upon the bushes like apples or oranges, felt it a pleasing duty to charge his ill adventure upon Columbus, and to crush him by every means however unfair, unmanly, unmerciful, ungenerous or ungodly. Between these various millstones of destruction, Columbus was ground to powder. It must also be confessed, that from and after his first voyage he had not, or did not, exhibit much of those qualities which are absolutely essential in an executive officer, in so vast and difficult an enterprise. From that time forward, insubordination and failure kept him close companionship.

In its effect and results, it made but little difference whether Columbus could not govern and control the colonists, or if the fact was that they would not submit to or be governed by him; in either case the results would be the same to Columbus, and equally disastrous to him. As a bold explorer he was courageous and superb; but as a successful colonizer, for the reasons already indicated, he was a decided failure.

CHAPTER XIII.

IN justice to Columbus, we will do well to remember that the average pioneer gold seeker or gold digger, who leaves home and country, parents, wife and children, to gather the auriferous dust, unrestrained by the proprieties of home, the heavenly influence of woman, regardless of a citizen's duty or a subject's loyalty, was mainly the material out of which Columbus was expected to construct orderly society and law-respecting colonies. Failure under such circumstances (either then or now), may be reasonably anticipated. Final success is nearly always at the cost of blood.

Nearly every historian who has written upon the subject, has felt the necessity of making some explanation to his readers for the downfall of Columbus. The desire is quite inevitable, but the reasons assigned are as various and contradictory as they usually are in similar cases, and not more so. Those who would inordinately magnify the merits of Columbus, must necessarily impugn the motives and obscure the merits of the sovereigns and many other worthy persons. Those who are interested in pushing into undue prominence the great virtues and merits of the sovereigns, or of the co-laborers of Columbus, in the great undertaking, are obliged to do so, somewhat to the detriment of the fame of Columbus. Possibly mankind is too prone to impugn and impeach the best intentions and motives of those whose fortune it is to be leaders or actors in any great enterprise. It is just as easy, more Christian-like and charitable, to assume that all parties acted well their parts, from the best of motives and in the exercise of their best judgment, at the same time also with a due personal regard for their own interests and advantage. Men would cease to be men upon any other theory.

CHAPTER XIV.

THE exploration of the continent of America was a slow process, and was not fully completed in 200 years from the time of the first discovery.

The remaining facts, in the exploration of America, are but the continuation of the work auspiciously inaugurated by Columbus.

When news spread through Europe that Columbus had successfully overcome and mastered the real and imaginary dangers of the Atlantic, and had, as was then believed, been to Asia, numerous expeditions, and by various nations, were sent out in search of the wealth of the newly discovered land. Some sailed in a more northerly, others in a more southerly direction, all reaching land, and within a few years the truth began to dawn, and it was ascertained that Columbus, after all, had been mistaken as to the size of the earth and as to his having reached Asia. The greater the extent of the explorations the less the matter tallied with the grandeur, riches and wealth described by Marco Polo. The inhabitants were nearly all naked, without learning or property, living in a decidedly primitive and savage state. The extent and contour of the new land was unknown, and it early became the grand aim to find a passage or strait through to regions beyond. Such a passage was sought for from Labrador, in the north, to Patagonia, at the south, but could not be found anywhere. The fact was now partly surmised, that Asia had not been found. Doubts had even been expressed before the death of Columbus, and as the enormous riches believed to exist in the oriental kingdom, were not found, the fame of Columbus, as the discoverer of Asia, by the west, began to wane.

Admiral Vasco Nunez, generally known as "Balboa," more than seven years after the death of Columbus, and a year and a half after the death of Vespucius, to wit, September 25th, 1513, from the summit of Darien, was the first civilized man to behold the grand secret of the age, *the Pacific Ocean*, separating the newly discovered continent from Asia. He named the waters "Mar del Sur," in English, "South Sea," afterwards named "Pacific Ocean," by Magellan, who first sailed across its waters, from the west towards the east.

Here then appeared a new problem for solution, raised by the discovery of Balboa, to wit, the breadth of the newly discovered waters and the remaining distance to Asia, whose splendors and riches all Europe was seeking.

Bartholomew Diaz, in the interest of Portugal, in 1486, had doubled the Cape of Good Hope, at the southern extremity of Africa, demonstrating the possibility of circumnavigating that continent. He returned to Lisbon in 1487. Following up the discovery of Diaz, Vasco da Gama sailed from Lisbon, July 8th, 1497, with a fleet of five vessels, in the interval between the second and third voyages of Columbus. He doubled Cape of Good Hope in the following November, and reached Calicut in India, May 20th, 1498, a few days before Columbus sailed on his third voyage. Thus the Portuguese had accomplished the end Columbus had in view, and reached the land

and countries Columbus was doomed never to behold.

A writer remarks, "that while the Portuguese took the right way by the east and reached Asia, Columbus took the wrong way and discovered America."

The absolute demonstration of the sphericity of the earth or its circumnavigation was yet unaccomplished, and the breadth of the Pacific Ocean as yet unknown.

In 1519, Magellan, who had been offended by Portugal and had removed to Spain, at once entered in the interest of Spain, upon the greatest voyage that had ever until then, or has since, been performed by any navigator. He started from the Canary Islands, where the trans-Atlantic voyages generally commenced, and sailed thence southwesterly across the Atlantic Ocean to the east coast of Brazil, thence southward along the eastern coast of South America to the strait bearing his name, separating the continent of South America from the Island Terra del Fuego, thence through the strait and northerly along the west coast to the latitude of twenty degrees south, thence west and northwest across the Pacific Ocean to the Phillipine Islands, where in a battle he lost his life. But his voyage was completed by his lieutenant, Sebastian del Cano, southerly through the China Sea, westerly across the Indian Ocean, thence southerly around the south of Africa, thence northerly along the west coast of Africa to Spain, arriving home September 6th, 1522, having sailed by their reckoning 43,000 miles. Much inferior voyages seem to have somewhat eclipsed the magnitude of this stupendous voyage of Magellan, or caused it to be either underestimated, or at least to slumber in comparative obscurity and forgetfulness. As compared with any preceding navigation, the length, daring, duration, dangers, sufferings and vicissitudes of that voyage, as well as its scientific, geographic, commercial results and utility, make all former voyages appear quite insignificant. The few survivors who returned to Spain, must have entertained very different notions of the size of the earth, from the sailors under Columbus. They were the first men to grasp and appreciate true and substantial notions involved in the physical demonstration of the sphericity of the earth.

Thus at the end of 2000 years, the theories of old Thales, Pythagoras and Eratosthenes were proved: the earth is a sphere, and its circumference is nearly 25,000 miles. Verily, Diaz, Da Gama, Columbus and Magellan, are great names of great men in the world's history. The ripened fruits of the first voyage of Columbus were thus at length gathered.

The first voyage of Columbus opened the gates to a knowledge of nearly one-half of the surface of the earth. From Europe the nearly direct westerly voyage to Asia will be possible, when the Isthmus of Darien, like Suez, is severed by a ship canal, and not before. A voyage by the route of Magellan, is too devious, tedious and long for the purposes of profitable commerce.

Our debt of gratitude is the due of Columbus. In the ages yet to come, among the long list of moral, mental, political or military heroes, whose names the world has delighted in emblazoning on the escutcheon of fame, will shine with an ever increasing lustre, the name of America's discoverer. We can but experience a feeling of regret, that this great benefactor of our race passed to his grave in utter ignorance of the grandeur of his discovery. Meager indeed by comparison would it have been, had he reached Asia and missed the discovery of this continent. At this distance of time, his entire failure to realize the object and purposes of his voyage to the west, is quite obscured and almost forgotten by the grand circumstance of his accidental discovery of America. Fears have been entertained by some, that the name of Columbus is to be placed in the calendar of saints, and this for the past few years appears to have induced ungenerous attacks upon his private life and public character, and to disparage his merits as the American discoverer.

The power to canonize is vested in an entirely competent tribunal, and with its deliberation or determinations most people are unable to see any cause for alarm. If the body, which alone has the power to pass upon the question, shall in its wisdom deem it meet to place the name of Columbus ever so conspicuously upon the saintly calendar, it is difficult to conceive, why it should be cause for offence to any human being. The expensive and elaborate preparations now being put forth for an international, everlasting and grateful testimony in honor of his name and fame, for discovering to civilization and Christianity the American continent, entirely precludes the possibility of a handful of pessimistic grumblers, at this late day, of transferring his glory to any other of the sons of men.

Truth and justice should be the ultimatum of the historian, and he monstrously fails in his public duty, who pre-determines to unduly exalt any character to the disparaging of any other, or depreciates a character with the intent that another may appear in better historic garb.

The fame of Columbus is grounded upon the planning and execution of his first voyage across the Atlantic Ocean, and his crowning glory is not diminished because the dangers apprehended were purely imaginary and unreal. His name may not be invulnerable to the onslaughts of a just criticism, otherwise he were more than human. We can now see as well as it must have been, even then, that a trans-Atlantic voyage was as easy, safe and simple as the longitudinal voyages of the Mediterranean Sea. We may wonder why ages upon ages passed, without producing a man possessed of the faith, courage and skill to attempt the voyage. We may ponder or query to know, why the Christian revelation was postponed or withheld from the earlier ages, or why public sentiment so long countenanced human slavery, or why a Stephenson, a Fulton, a Morse, or an Edison, were not forthcoming until the nineteenth century? Human wit or wisdom cannot solve these questions. Men may know the fact, God alone the reason.

As the discoverer of America, the public character and achievements of Columbus alone concern us. As a private individual, he is entitled to be estimated and judged by the standard of ethics of his own day and generation, and not by a code recognized and approved 400 years later. The world has been slow to acknowledge and emphasize the utility of his life and labor by a just and public recognition. But the better qualities of generosity and judgment are at the end of 400 years to give world-wide and ample expression. The crowning event of a prolonged series of centennary celebrations (now somewhat threadbare), will be closed by an international commemoration of the four hundredth anniversary of the discovery of America by Christopher Columbus.

The magnitude and importance of that discovery entirely overshadows all merely local or national events. In every sense it has been and is a matter of international and world-wide moment, and in its immediate and remote consequences and effects upon the happiness, well-being and expansion of mankind, fairly transcends every other event in the history of the world.

Surely Americans, and particularly citizens of the United States, will appreciate the distinguished honor of having the world's commemorative proceedings focused in the midst of their great domain, and greet with a royal welcome the visiting nations, whose people have from time to time chosen this land for their home, and now constitute a nation of freemen.

www.ingramcontent.com/pod-product-compliance
Lightning Source LLC
Chambersburg PA
CBHW022134160426
43197CB00009B/1282